CONSERVATION CANINES

How Dogs Work for the Environment

Foreword by Anjelica Huston

Text and photographs by
ISABELLE GROC

ORCA BOOK PUBLISHERS

Published in Canada and the United States
in 2021 by Orca Book Publishers.
orcabook.com

Library and Archives Canada Cataloguing in Publication
Title: Conservation canines : how dogs work for the environment /
text and photographs by Isabelle Groc.
Names: Groc, Isabelle, author, photographer.
Series: Orca wild ; 7.
Description: Series statement: Orca wild ; 7 |
Includes bibliographical references.
Identifiers: Canadiana (print) 20210095326 |
Canadiana (ebook) 20210095377 | ISBN 9781459821606 (hardcover) |
ISBN 9781459821613 (PDF) | ISBN 9781459821620 (EPUB)
Subjects: LCSH: Working dogs—Juvenile literature. |
LCSH: Human-animal relationships—Juvenile literature. |
LCSH: Environmental protection—Juvenile literature. |
LCSH: Wildlife conservation—Juvenile literature.
Classification: LCC SF428.2 .G76 2021 | DDC j636.7/0886—dc23

Library of Congress Control Number: 2020951461

Summary: This nonfiction book for middle readers examines
the lives of dogs who work with humans to find new ways to solve
environmental problems. Included are stories of dog encounters in
the field and examples of canines working to conserve wildlife.

Orca Book Publishers is committed to reducing
the consumption of nonrenewable resources in the
making of our books. We make every effort to use
materials that support a sustainable future.

Orca Book Publishers gratefully acknowledges the support
for its publishing programs provided by the following
agencies: the Government of Canada, the Canada Council
for the Arts and the Province of British Columbia through
the BC Arts Council and the Book Publishing Tax Credit.

Front and back cover photos by Isabelle Groc
Edited by Sarah N. Harvey
Foreword by Anjelica Huston
Design by Dahlia Yuen

Printed and bound in China.

24 23 22 21 • 1 2 3 4

Cheetah Conservation Fund's detection dog
Levi is rewarded with a play session after finding
cheetah poop in a vast tract of land in Namibia.

For all canines, the people who love them, and my parents.

CONTENTS

1

A BRIEF HISTORY OF THE WORKING DOG

2

WILDLIFE GUARDIANS AND PEACEMAKERS

3
A NOSE FOR CONSERVATION

4
TOP DOGS SAVING THE WILD

5
DOGS AND HUMANS: PARTNERS IN CONSERVATION

Ayla, an Anatolian shepherd, is one of
Anjelica Huston's three dogs. BLAKE BASHOFF

FOREWORD

I have loved dogs for as long as I can remember and was lucky to have grown up with a great variety of canine friends. There was my father's regal Irish wolfhound, Seamus, who stood at seven feet on his hind paws and actually allowed my brother and me to ride him as children. Moses, a beautiful golden sheepdog we rescued from drowning in a river as a tiny puppy. My brother's Llewellin setter with the sad eyes, a hunting dog named Flash who followed him devotedly through bogs and marshes in the west of Ireland. And there was my puppy Mindy, a miniature poodle—the first dog I could call my own. She was my sole responsibility and the love of my life. Dogs were my teachers. They taught me about love and loyalty, faithfulness and patience, and, most of all, true, unconditional friendship.

I have always had dogs in my life, and I rate their fellowship as highly as I would any human relationship. Currently I am the proud owner of three beautiful dogs—a little mutt of fourteen called Pootie, a fox terrier named Oscar, whom I inherited from a dear friend, and Ayla, a magnificent Anatolian shepherd who is the livestock guardian at my farm and guardian of her herd of Toggenburg goats.

I am so happy that *Conservation Canines: How Dogs Work for the Environment* showcases not just what dogs do for us as people, but also what they do for our planet. With their keen noses and highly developed senses, dogs are working with conservationists more and more to help collect information that assists with wildlife protection—from finding endangered animals and plants to locating unwanted or harmful species to helping reduce human–wildlife conflict.

With bold, colorful photographs by author Isabelle Groc that match the stories of the canine heroes we meet throughout the book, this amazing resource is suitable for children and adults alike to teach us about dog conservationists. The stories of these conservation canines celebrate the profound and ancestral human–animal bond, and give hope and inspiration to us all for finding new ways for people to coexist with wildlife and protect the natural world.

There is much to learn and, with the help of our four-legged friends, far more to achieve.

—**Anjelica Huston,**
Actor and Author

Australian cattle dog Alli is looking for the elusive Oregon spotted frog in a wetland of British Columbia, working alongside her human partner, Heath Smith. Alli used to be a drug-detection dog before taking on her job in conservation. "It was love at first sight," Smith says of his first meeting with her.

INTRODUCTION

Alli moved swiftly over the spongy earth, cutting a sharp path through the knee-high grass of a *wetland* in the Fraser Valley, a couple of hours' drive from Vancouver, British Columbia. Behind her, Monica Pearson, a conservation biologist, and Heath Smith, Alli's trainer, followed in hot pursuit. But Alli paid them no mind. Ears pricked and nose to the ground, the energetic Australian cattle dog was on a mission. Just as she approached the edge of a nearby pond, Alli stopped suddenly and lay down. She looked over at Smith, fixing him with a gaze that radiated both intensity and expectation. Smith and Pearson approached the dog, and Smith knelt down and started digging through the grass. Within a few seconds he uncovered what had made Alli stop—a small frog with golden eyes. "Yeah!" Pearson exclaimed, turning to Alli. "Good girl."

Mission accomplished. Smith reached into his pocket, pulled out a ball and rewarded Alli with a spirited game of fetch. Pearson, meanwhile, focused on the frog, measuring its body length, checking its weight and attaching a small transmitter belt.

This was no ordinary frog. It was an Oregon spotted frog (*Rana pretiosa*, or "precious frog"), one of Canada's most endangered *amphibians*—and one of the most difficult to find. In Canada, the Oregon spotted frog is found only in British Columbia's Fraser Valley. Just 400 to 700 frogs are left, distributed in six isolated populations. Their numbers have declined by as much as 90 percent, mostly because of the loss of their wetland *habitat* to agriculture and urban development. Understanding where the frogs live is critical to their long-term survival. When new populations are discovered, wildlife managers can take steps to protect the habitat and reduce threats.

The endangered Oregon spotted frog survives in only a handful of wetlands in British Columbia.

But finding new populations of Oregon spotted frogs in wetlands is a time-consuming and unreliable process, mainly because it is difficult for people to move through these environments. Surveyors walk slowly in knee-deep mud during the short frog-breeding season and can easily miss seeing the frogs. With skin ranging from olive green to dark or reddish brown, the Oregon spotted frog is well camouflaged. It spends most of its time underwater and is expert at hiding under vegetation and in tunnels. Pearson has spent years studying the frogs, but when she looks for them in their unstable, spongy, muddy habitat, it can take her hours to find one.

This changed when Alli came along in March 2012 to help find the shy frogs. When I met Alli for the first time, she was a veteran member of the Conservation Canines program at the University of Washington in Seattle, which trains dogs to use their keen sense of smell to help find threatened and *endangered species*. Alli is nimble and fast, able to cover large areas in a short period of time, and her acute sense of smell allows her to catch the scent of a *species* quickly.

Around the world, many more dogs like Alli are taking on conservation jobs. With their precise sense of smell, hard-working temperament and ability to *bond* with humans, dogs have long been valued for helping with difficult tasks such as searching for drugs and explosives or locating missing persons. Throughout history, dogs have also been placed in working roles to interact with wildlife as hunting dogs or *livestock guardian dogs*.

But today *canine* skills are increasingly being put to work in a variety of wildlife conservation projects to help the world's most vulnerable species. With growing pressure on the environment and many species on the brink of *extinction*, Alli and other dogs are taking on new roles at unprecedented levels, helping wildlife one sniff and bark at a time.

As detection dogs, they work in different types of environments, from oceans to deserts, jungles and forests to wetlands. They find animal poop, track down elusive species, help enforce environmental protection laws, detect illegally obtained wildlife products such as rhino horns, shark fins and elephant ivory, and even catch people who are *poaching*. They assist in controlling *invasive species* that harm native environments and species.

With the return of *predators* such as wolves and bears in different parts of the world, livestock guardian dogs are once again working alongside humans. They keep wolves, bears and cheetahs away from goats, sheep and cattle, which means people and predators have a better chance of living together peacefully on the same land.

In this book you will get to know some of the four-legged conservation heroes who tirelessly work to help wildlife around the world. You'll also meet the people teaming up with them to make a difference. You will learn what kind of training dogs need to work in wildlife conservation, and you will follow them in the field and discover how their noses help scientists, *conservationists*, ranchers and farmers solve some of our most urgent environmental problems.

Humans and dogs have had a special relationship for thousands of years. Today this unique bond between people and canines helps us better understand and protect endangered wildlife species on the planet we all share.

Conservation dog Alli had never smelled a frog before. Yet she successfully detected one underwater in no time. "She is a quick learner," handler Heath Smith says.

In Namibia, Spots, a Kangal shepherd, works with Armas Shaanika, Cheetah Conservation Fund's chief goat herder, to protect livestock from predators when herds graze on open farmlands.

1

A BRIEF HISTORY OF THE WORKING DOG

I was once walking on a remote beach on Vancouver Island in British Columbia when I encountered a coastal wolf feeding on the shoreline. For a short moment we both stood still, looking into each other's eyes. I was taken aback by the mix of emotions I experienced. I was standing in front of a wild animal, yet this wolf seemed strangely familiar, and I felt surprisingly close to it. Its posture and gaze reminded me of our cherished animal companion, the dog. The encounter lasted for only a few minutes, and then the wolf walked away into the forest.

I often recall this encounter when I consider the ancient relationship between humans and wolves. Dogs, our closest friends in the animal kingdom and the ones who support us in so many ways, were once wolves. Dogs came from the wild to live with humans. They are able to communicate with us in ways we rarely experience with other animals. Perhaps because they create a bridge between the human world and the wild, dogs are in the best position to do work that helps us in our interactions with wild animals, whether it is to protect humans and farm animals from predators, understand the natural world or conserve endangered species.

A coastal wolf scans the environment on Vancouver Island, BC.

The special qualities of our four-legged companions have been acknowledged for thousands of years, and to this day humans are still discovering jobs that dogs can do.

FROM WOLF TO DOG

A long time ago dogs were wolves, and today the closest living relative of the dog is the gray wolf (*Canis lupus*). Because dogs and present-day wolves share a common ancestor, they can be viewed as "cousins." How and when some wolves became dogs is not known for certain. One theory is that when humans established permanent settlements, their activities produced food waste, which became an easy food source for individual wolves who were not afraid of humans. Over time wolves became used to living with people, and humans began to tolerate them as well. It is also possible that some humans raised wolf cubs. The process of *domestication* happened over many generations as ancient wolf lineages

Wolf-dog Tundra and her owner, Gary Allan, meet children on a walk on Vancouver Island, BC.

(a lineage is a group of individuals descending from a common ancestor) adapted to humans, becoming more and more tame. Eventually they had become distinct from their wild ancestors in both behavior and appearance. Meanwhile, the other wolves stayed wild, and these are the wolves that still live in the forests and other habitats today.

Dogs were the first domesticated animal, and scientists believe this domestication occurred about 14,000 to 40,000 years ago in Europe or East Asia. Archaeological evidence of canines and humans being buried together 14,000 years ago indicates the close bond that existed between people and dogs even at that time. Modern dog *breeds* are a product of the last 200 years, and there is now incredible diversity in the animals' size, shape and behavior. There are nearly 400 breeds today, and dogs are by far the planet's most abundant *carnivore*, with an estimated population of 900 million.

Dogs have been people's companions for thousands of years.

A WOLF IN DOG'S CLOTHING?

During the summer of 2018, locals found the remains of an 18,000-year-old puppy buried in a frozen lump of mud near Yakutsk, a city in eastern Siberia, Russia. Preserved by permafrost, the animal's parts were remarkably intact, including its nose, fur, whiskers and teeth. Researchers suggest the animal was just two months old when it died, although they do not know the cause of death. What is intriguing about this discovery is that the scientists who conducted initial *DNA* tests were not able to define the puppy as a wolf, dog or wolf-dog, which shows there is still much to learn about the origin of dogs. Further tests might provide more insight into exactly when dogs were domesticated. In the meantime, since it has been established that the puppy is a male, the scientists have named him Dogor, which means "friend" in the Yakut language.

Modern dogs are descendants of wolves.
JAMES GRITZ AND R A KEARTON/GETTY IMAGES

THE FIRST WORKING DOGS

As wolves transformed into dogs, they became closely integrated with humans' lives, in more ways than any other animal. People discovered dogs' potential as working companions in a variety of environments. Ancient drawings, sculptures and rock carvings dating back 4,000 to 9,000 years suggest that humans used dogs in working roles such as *herding*, hunting and guarding. In Europe and Asia during this time, dogs helped shepherds protect their goats and sheep from predators such as brown bears, lynxes and gray wolves.

Larane, a Kangal shepherd, watches over a sheep herd on an organic cheese farm in southwest France. Owners Raymonde Etcharry and Alain Domini have nine livestock guardian dogs (Kangals and patous) who help protect their animals from stray dogs and bears.

Traditionally, early working canines did not belong to a specific breed. They were village dogs, not owned by anyone in particular, who survived on food leftovers from the villagers. They warned people about potential intruders—in fact, alerting humans to danger was probably the very first job dogs took on. Dogs born in close proximity to livestock became comfortable living among sheep and goats and instinctively watched over them, making sure they were not taken by predators or thieves.

Dogs accompanied shepherds and flocks to different grazing areas on daily short journeys to a pasture or mountain, or on longer seasonal migrations that could take several months, traveling along valleys and across mountains to get from winter to summer grazing areas, a movement called *transhumance*. Shepherds selected those dogs with behaviors and physical characteristics that made them good at their jobs, and over time the dogs developed into specific breeds with those attributes. The dogs were often large, with big heads.

The practice of keeping livestock guardian dogs spread into many regions, thanks initially to the migration of nomadic peoples, who traveled with dogs. Today there are approximately 50 recognized breeds of livestock guardian dogs. Most come from Europe and Asia, are specific to a single country or region and are adapted to different environments and the needs of local shepherds. Their colors and hair coats vary, but they have certain qualities in common: in addition to their large size (meant to impress predators), they are trustworthy, protective and attentive to the flock or herd. You will learn more about guarding canines in chapter 2.

In Central Portugal, a farmer interacts with a Spanish mastiff, a large livestock guardian dog who helps protect sheep against predator attacks.

Wildlife-detection dog Benny searches cargo for illegal wildlife products hidden by Detective Lauren Wendt at the Port of Tacoma in Washington State.

A NOSE AT WORK

While dogs were recognized thousands of years ago for their unique ability to protect people and livestock against wild predators, humans also discovered that dogs' noses were vastly more sensitive than their own and could be put to work. Dogs have helped humans hunt for food for centuries, but in the last hundred years conservationists and scientists realized that the dog's extraordinary sense of smell could help them in wildlife research and conservation, and that dogs could be trained to sniff out just about anything.

New Zealand was the first country to employ canines for wildlife conservation, in the 1890s. Early conservationist Richard Henry relied on his dog's powerful sense of smell to track and locate the kiwi and the kakapo, two fragile species of flightless birds that Henry wanted to move to an island where they would be safe from predators. Since that time, dogs of all kinds have been used to help wildlife around the world, detecting anything that emits a scent.

NOSE POWER

A dog's sense of smell develops during the first two weeks of its life. Puppies can even learn scents before they are born. People often assume that a dog's nose is many times more sensitive than a human's. In fact, when a range of odors is tested, humans outperform dogs in detecting some smells while being less sensitive to others. Certain dogs, such as bloodhounds, have been bred specifically to detect scents, but it is still not known how much better they are at this compared to other dogs. One study suggested traditional scent dogs may be better, and another showed that

DOG ON DUTY:
TRUFFLE HUNTER

Truffles, one of our most expensive treats, grow underground at the base of trees. When humans use a rake to harvest truffles, they get worthless unripe truffles along with the ripe ones. They also rip up the roots and soil, which can cause serious damage to the trees and other forest organisms. Dogs' noses are so sensitive that they can be trained to find ripe truffles. In Europe the traditional truffle dog is the lagotto Romagnolo, an Italian breed that looks a bit like a standard poodle, but any dog can be trained to hunt truffles.

A dog is trained for truffle hunting in the San Miniato area in Tuscany, Italy, a region well known for white truffles. GUIDO COZZI/ ATLANTIDE PHOTOTRAVEL/GETTY IMAGES

A pug searches through the snow.
TANJA ESSER / EYEEM/GETTY IMAGES

pugs beat German shepherds at detecting a target odor. In reality, for the many people who work with scent detection dogs, the key factor is how humans interact and communicate with the dogs.

THE SNIFFING ACT

Sniffing is the action of inhaling air. We all sniff, whether it is to smell fresh waffles in the morning, the grass after a rain or what's cooking for dinner. Animals also sniff, to explore the world around them, to find food, water and companions, and to avoid predators. African elephants have by far the highest number of genes associated with *olfactory* reception (ability to detect odors) of any animal species—2,000 functional genes, which is over twice the number found in dogs (about 800). However, scientists have found that having more olfactory *receptors* does not necessarily indicate a better sense of smell. Some have argued that the extra receptors may help fine-tune the ability to smell the specific types of chemicals necessary for the animals, but more research is needed.

So what happens when a dog sniffs? A dog can inhale air rapidly, and it all begins with muscles in the nostrils straining to draw a current of air into them. Every living thing, plant or animal, releases a unique odor. When the dog sniffs, scent molecules—tiny chemicals—reach the deeper parts of the nose cavity.

Dogs have a large nose cavity that contains a structure made of a complex system of small bony walls. This large surface is covered by the *olfactory epithelium*, which is the sensing tissue that processes the molecules reaching the nose cavity. The dog is able to distinguish between a large number of different scents because the olfactory

African elephants have the most olfactory reception genes ever identified in a single species.

epithelium holds an extraordinary number of different types of olfactory receptors, each equipped with proteins to help catch molecules of certain shapes and identify them.

While human noses possess about 6 million olfactory receptor neurons, dogs have an estimated 125 to 300 million, which means dogs are able to detect many kinds of smells, even when they are faint.

In her book *Inside of a Dog: What Dogs See, Smell, and Know*, dog-behavior specialist Alexandra Horowitz provides her own interpretation of how humans and dogs experience a rose. To a dog, every detail that we see has a corresponding smell, from the pollen left on a petal by an insect to a dewdrop on a thorn. "While we can see one of the petals drying and browning, the dog can smell this process of decay and aging. Imagine smelling every minute visual detail. That might be the experience of a rose to a dog," she writes.

This sense of smell makes dogs ideal working companions for people. They can be trained to detect multiple and specific odors at very small concentrations and seek them simultaneously. And dogs have additional qualities that make them exceptional work partners. They are agile and can move easily in terrains hard for humans to access in order to locate the source of the odor. Perhaps most important is their unique capacity to communicate and cooperate with humans. Our hardworking, furry friends are always eager to please us, and we can teach them to communicate the information they acquire with their noses.

WHAT DOGS SEE AND HEAR

Dogs have an extraordinary sense of smell, but what about their other senses? Do they use those as expertly while they work alongside humans? The dog's retina consists of two types of specific receptor cells, which are most sensitive to colors that humans see as blue-violet and greenish yellow. Dogs can easily distinguish between yellowish and bluish objects, but they don't see reddish colors, instead perceiving them as gray.

Casey, a wirehaired Jack Russell terrier, was rescued from the Kitsap Humane Society and now works in the University of Washington's Conservation Canines program.

Pips is a handsome Australian cattle dog who had been adopted and returned to an animal shelter three times before he found a new purpose in life as a Conservation Canine.

Perhaps because they are the descendants of wolves, dogs have hearing abilities that are particularly useful to a predator on a hunt. For example, dogs are capable of detecting small movements from a long distance that humans cannot see. People find this skill useful for hunting, as their dogs can easily locate small *prey* animals.

Dogs are able to rotate their ears in order to determine the direction a sound is coming from—kind of like adjusting a satellite dish. Their hearing range is much broader than that of humans. While dogs and humans hear deep, low-frequency sounds (ranging between 64 and 67 Hz or hertz—hertz is a standard measure of frequency) equally, dogs can hear far higher frequencies (45,000 Hz) than we can—our maximum is about 20,000 Hz. It means dogs can probably hear the high-frequency vocalizations of small rodents such as rats and mice. This hearing ability makes it easier to hunt these animals, which often make high-pitched calls when moving.

Great Pyrenees Jougnette guards livestock in a pasture at Mathieu Mauriès's farm, Hogan des Vents, in southwest France.

2

WILDLIFE GUARDIANS AND PEACEMAKERS

Even though they had worked alongside shepherds to protect livestock for millennia, most livestock guardian dogs lost their jobs in the 19th and 20th centuries. In some parts of Europe, humans systematically persecuted great predators, and with wolves and bears gone from the landscape, shepherds no longer needed to keep livestock guardian dogs. But as these predators make a comeback in various parts of the world, specially trained canines are again being called for duty. And now the job description has expanded to include protecting vulnerable wildlife.

LIVING WITH PREDATORS
THE RETURN OF WOLVES AND BEARS

Historically in Europe and North America, predators that came near people's livestock were hunted, poisoned and trapped—and sometimes they still are today. In Europe, wolves and bears were persecuted to the point that they had disappeared from many regions by the 19th and 20th centuries. Their habitat had diminished due to the expansion of agriculture, forestry and human settlements.

Wolves are slowly recolonizing Vancouver Island, after several attempts to get rid of the wolf population in this region of British Columbia.

The wolf was (and still is) revered by many of the Indigenous Peoples of North America, but when European settlers arrived, they brought with them negative attitudes toward predators. They not only killed wolves and bears, but also eradicated wild prey such as deer and turkeys, destroying their habitats to make room for human settlements and livestock. Government agencies initiated bounty programs, paying hunters to kill wolves. In Canada, 60,000 wolves now occupy about 90 percent of their historic *range*, but wolf hunting is still legal.

By the middle of the 20th century, nearly all gray wolves had disappeared from the lower 48 adjoining states in the United States. Only a small population of about 100 wolves remained in northeastern Minnesota and Isle Royale National Park in Michigan.

Wolves started to naturally recolonize their territories in Minnesota, Wisconsin and Michigan in the 1970s. After receiving federal protections, and with reintroduction programs (for example, wolves were brought back to Yellowstone National Park in 1995 and 1996), about 6,000 wolves now occupy about 10 percent of their historic range in the lower 48 states.

Since the reintroduction of wolves to Yellowstone, many millions of people have visited, and the appreciation of wolves has only grown. Some visitors enjoy seeing them or hearing them howl, while others are simply happy that the wolf population is on the rise. Today wolves roam in parts of 12 states, and public-opinion surveys show they are overwhelmingly popular.

When the grizzly bear was listed under the Endangered Species Act in 1975, its population in the lower 48 was down to fewer than 1,000 animals. Today about 1,500 grizzly bears occupy less than 2 percent of their former range in the lower 48. In the Greater Yellowstone Ecosystem, an area that includes Yellowstone National Park, their population has increased from 136 in 1975 to more than 700. There are about 26,000 grizzly bears in Canada, with more than half (16,000) found in British Columbia and the rest in Alberta and the three territories.

In Europe, following generations of persecution by humans, large predators are now protected by law at national and international levels. Most bear populations are strictly protected and so are wolves, with some exceptions.

Gray wolves are now recovering in such places as the French Alps, the Jura Mountains (France/Switzerland), the Iberian Peninsula (Spain/Portugal), Central Europe and Scandinavia. Brown bears are also reestablishing in the Pyrenees Mountains (France/Spain), due to reintroduction programs.

Conservationists celebrate the return of these great predators because they play an important role in the *ecosystem*, symbolize wilderness and offer hope in the face of the extinction crisis. Since wolves were reintroduced to Yellowstone National Park, scientists have discovered their

The end of widespread persecution and the introduction of protection measures have allowed grizzly bear populations to recover and expand in many areas of North America.

influence as a keystone species. Wolves started preying on the elk population, which had increased significantly in the absence of predators. With fewer elk grazing, the grass, shrubs and trees flourished and spread. Willows returned to the riverbanks. As a result, beavers had more material for building their dams, which in turn created habitat for fish, reptiles and other animals. In Wisconsin, scientists have shown that since wolves have returned, rare understory plants (which grow beneath the main canopy of a forest) are recovering from the damage caused by overabundant deer. Wolves help reduce the number of deer and their negative impacts on crops and ornamental garden plants and in collisions with vehicles. Grizzly bears also play a key ecological role in reducing the growth of ungulate populations such as moose and other herbivores that can damage vegetation if they overbrowse an ecosystem.

Despite all the benefits that large carnivores bring to the landscape, anti-predator attitudes persist. When they return to their former territories, either through natural colonization or reintroduction programs, large carnivores often share the landscape with livestock. Even though livestock losses due to predators are less than 1 percent of all livestock losses in the United States per year, most farmers who raise sheep and cattle continue to view large carnivores as threats to their livelihoods.

REDISCOVERING LIVESTOCK GUARDIAN DOGS

The lack of predators in some regions of Europe put guardian dogs out of work for a long time. Farmers had no need of them, plus many dogs were killed during the two world wars. The traditional knowledge of how to raise and

The Great Pyrenees, called a patou in France, is a strong mountain dog known for its patience and courage when defending livestock against predators. In the 17th century, the Great Pyrenees was adopted as the Royal Dog of France in the court of King Louis XIV.

Named after a football player, Táquara is a Portuguese Estrela mountain dog who, along with three other livestock guardian dogs, protects a goat herd owned by shepherd Dimas da Silva Paiva, as the animals move from a village to a mountain pasture in Central Portugal.

train the dogs was not passed on to younger generations of livestock producers. In some cases, ancient guardian dog breeds almost went extinct at the same time the predators they had been guarding against did, or they persisted only as pets.

Europeans immigrating to North America during the 1800s and 1900s did not bring knowledge of guardian dogs, nor did they incorporate them into their farming practices. Few livestock producers were actively using dogs before the 1970s.

Thanks to the work of some passionate individuals who revived the use of livestock guardian dogs and rediscovered the ancient working breeds, canine protectors are now coming back in force to help people make peace with predators.

Increasingly, in different regions of the world, dogs are being used to guard livestock. They are probably the most numerous of all the working dogs, with millions of them throughout the world. Since the return of the wolf in the French Alps, more than 3,000 dogs are now working there. In the United States, ranchers started using live-stock guardian dogs in the 1970s, when the government banned the use of a powerful poison that had been used to eliminate coyotes, the species responsible for most of the country's livestock losses. European dog breeds such as the akbash, komondor, Kangal shepherd, Maremma sheepdog and Great Pyrenees were sent to the United States, where they started patrolling lands in defense of livestock, needing little supervision. Dogs also proved their value in Canada, South America, Africa and Australia, protecting animals against all sorts of predators—wolves, coyotes, bears, cougars, lynxes, bobcats, wolverines, dingoes, chee-tahs, leopards, hyenas and even stray dogs.

A SPECIAL FRIENDSHIP

In the 19th century Charles Darwin joined the HMS *Beagle* as the ship's naturalist for a trip around the world. For five years the *Beagle* surveyed the coast of South America, and Darwin explored the continent and islands, writing obser-vations on animals, plants and everything else he saw. Darwin noticed working dogs in the countryside. "When riding, it is a common thing to meet a large flock of sheep guarded by one or two dogs, at the distance of some miles from any house or man. I often wondered how so firm a friendship had been established," he wrote in his book *The Voyage of the Beagle*.

Becoming a good livestock guardian dog starts with a special friendship. The dogs are raised from an early age with the animals they will be protecting. They learn to identify with their smell, and eventually the goats, sheep

Mathieu Mauriès, who breeds livestock guardian dogs, holds a three-month-old Great Pyrenees puppy on his farm in southwest France.

or cattle become the dog's family. The process is called *socialization*. Because of this strong friendship, the dogs show protective behavior toward "their" animals for the rest of their lives.

Raising a successful working dog takes knowledge and experience. A good dog can turn into a bad dog if not raised in the proper environment. It can misbehave, run away or chase wild animals other than predators.

Although a guardian dog is expected to work full-time with the livestock and largely unsupervised, the rancher or shepherd must still spend time with the dog. But it must be the right amount of time. With too much human contact at an early age, the pup will bond to humans, and its relationship with the livestock may weaken. As an adult, such a dog may try to come back to the house or follow its owner during the day rather than staying with the livestock. If there is too little human contact, the dog will be afraid of people, may be difficult to catch or handle or could potentially be aggressive toward humans.

Once its friendship with the herd is firmly established, it is time for the livestock guardian dog to start working—usually when it is about two years of age. But what does that involve exactly? The dog does not move or herd livestock, the job of herding dogs such as border collies.

Its only job is to stand guard, keeping predators from harming any members of the herd or flock. The dog places itself between the herd and the threat, barking loudly. If the predator persists, the dog will chase it away, but often the mere presence of an intimidating guardian is enough to make the predator leave. The dog remains with the herd even in the absence of the shepherd or rancher. Always alert and confident, the dog can quickly detect a threat

In Central Portugal, shepherd Maria Fernanda Rodrigues trusts Lord, along with two other Estrela mountain dogs, to protect her sheep from wolf attacks.

and, without hesitation, adopt a defense strategy geared to the type of predator, whether it is a stray dog, a fox, a wolf, a bear, ill-intentioned humans or even crows and vultures. By barking and marking, the dog sets the boundaries of a territory and lets predators know they need to search elsewhere for food.

GUARDIAN DOGS AT WORK
THE CHEETAH AND THE DOG

It is still cool as Spots gets ready to start work in the morning. Calm and confident, the imposing light-brown Kangal shepherd dog is leading a herd of goats into a pasture. "He is always excited to go out with the goats," says Toivo Tyapa, small-livestock manager at the Cheetah Conservation Fund (CCF) in the Republic of Namibia, a country in southwest Africa.

In north-central Namibia, the goats graze every day on land where leopards, cheetahs and jackals also live. But Spots keeps the goats safe. He watches over them intently, and if a predator approaches, he barks loudly and places

Cheetah Conservation Fund's Spots is a Kangal shepherd, a breed known for being attentive, fiercely protective of livestock animals and having an exceptionally loud bark that keeps predators away.

himself between the herd and the threatening animal. This is usually sufficient to scare the predator away. "Our goats go out every day, and we have cheetahs roaming around, but I have never experienced losses from a cheetah," says Tyapa. "They know that this herd of goats is with a dog, so they don't bother coming any closer."

Spots is a livestock guardian dog, and like others around the world, his job is to protect domestic animals against native predators. This, in turn, reduces humans' perceived need to kill the predators, so the dogs are actually protecting both the domestic animals and the predators.

Cheetahs are the fastest land animals on earth. They are struggling in the race against extinction. Once found throughout Africa and in much of Asia, they numbered around 100,000 in 1900. Cheetahs now persist in only 9 percent of their historic range, and the global population is estimated at about 7,100. Namibia is part of the home range of the world's largest subpopulation, which is approximately 1,500 animals.

Cheetahs do not do well in protected areas like national parks and wildlife reserves, which contain high densities of other, more powerful predators such as lions, leopards and hyenas, which kill cheetahs' cubs and steal their prey. This is why most cheetahs in Africa live outside protected areas, in open spaces and on private farmland. There they face other dangers.

Cheetahs are highly vulnerable to human-wildlife conflicts.

Because they live close to humans raising cows, sheep and goats, cheetahs are often held responsible for livestock losses, and many Namibian farmers used to believe they had no other option but to kill the big cats to protect their herds. CCF estimates that between 1980 and 1990, more than 7,000 cheetahs were lost in this way,

Staff from Cheetah Conservation Fund's Livestock Guarding Dog program help care for puppies as they are being weaned and beginning to eat solid food. When they are about 10 weeks old, the puppies will be placed on farms to protect livestock.

cutting their population by almost half. Convinced that farmers and predators could coexist, CCF turned to dogs to reduce conflict between farmers and big cats.

Since 1994 the organization has been placing Kangal shepherd dogs (also known as Anatolian shepherds) on farms across Namibia to protect livestock against predators. Kangals were chosen because they have a 6,000-year history of guarding sheep and goats from wolves and bears in Turkey. Their short coats protect them from thorns and bushes and make it easier for them to adapt to changing temperatures, both hot and cold. Their independent nature means they don't need to have people with them to guard animals successfully. They can work in vast, open spaces and cover long distances with their herds every day.

The goats that Spots is watching over belong to the CCF's model farm, which has been set up to show farmers how livestock and wildlife can live in harmony through improved herd management and the use of guard dogs. The dogs are most effective if farmers take additional steps to protect their livestock. For example, they are encouraged to keep the animals in sleeping pens called kraals at night and to breed the livestock at one time of the year only so that the young can be raised in groups around the kraal until they are big enough to go out with the herd. CCF breeds and trains puppies at its headquarters in Otjiwarongo, three hours north of the capital city of Windhoek. At a young age, the dogs are placed in pens with goats to live and bond with them. Before long they are ready to start protecting goats and sheep on farms.

Once the dogs are placed, CCF researchers visit them regularly and monitor their behavior. They initially found that some of the dogs were not doing well—they were chasing other wildlife, staying at home instead of going out with the herd, or harassing or hurting livestock. The researchers realized they needed to provide more training to the farmers so they would know how to care for the dogs, watch their behaviors and correct them if needed.

Sadly, Spots passed away in 2018, but his legacy lives on. So far CCF has placed nearly 700 dogs on farms across the country. According to Dr. Laurie Marker, CCF's founder and executive director, livestock losses have been reduced by 80 to 100 percent on farms with guarding dogs. "I picked the Kangal dogs because they are independent thinkers," she says. "They don't need to be told by humans what to do. They are way smarter." Thanks to the dogs, the lives of hundreds of cheetahs and other predators have been saved in Namibia.

Dr. Laurie Marker, founder and executive director of Cheetah Conservation Fund, with a pair of five-week-old livestock guarding dog puppies. Marker began the LGD program in Namibia in 1994, and it continues to be one of CCF's most important programs to reduce human–carnivore conflict and the loss of cheetahs and other predators.

A rescued Iberian wolf at Grupo Lobo's Iberian Wolf Recovery Centre in Portugal.

Biologist Silvia Ribeiro with Estrela mountain dog Fidalga, whose name means "noblewoman" in Portuguese.

DOGS FACING WOLVES IN PORTUGAL

Spain and Portugal are home to nearly 15 percent of Europe's wolves. There are around 17,000 wolves in Europe (excluding Russia and Belarus and all of Ukraine apart from the Carpathians). In Portugal, there are now about 300 Iberian wolves—a subspecies of gray wolf also present in Spain. They are found only in the north and center of the country, which represents about 25 percent of their original range. As in other parts of Europe, wolves in Portugal were persecuted. They used to be found in the whole country, but their range was reduced by more than 80 percent.

Iberian wolves have been protected by Portuguese law since 1988, yet farmers continue to poison or shoot them. Because there are few ungulates such as deer for wolves to eat, they turn to cattle and goats for food, which can lead to conflict with people, especially in areas of recent wolf expansion, where livestock management is no longer adapted to the presence of wolves, or in specific areas with extensive cattle herds. A study of northern Portugal's Peneda-Gerês National Park, where domestic animals make up 90 percent of the wolves' diet, found that almost half of the known wolf deaths were a result of illegal shooting and poisoning.

A passionate biologist named Silvia Ribeiro wanted to change attitudes and promote peaceful coexistence between wolves, farmers and livestock. Through the wolf-conservation organization Grupo Lobo, she is encouraging farmers to turn back the clock and work with four ancient breeds of Portuguese guarding dog, raised in different regions of Portugal, that helped people coexist with wolves in the past—the cão da Serra da Estrela (aka Estrela mountain dog), the cão de Castro Laboreiro (aka Castro Laboreiro dog), the rafeiro do Alentejo (aka Alentejo mastiff) and the cão de Gado Transmontano (aka Transmontano mastiff).

Since 1997 Ribeiro has been giving guardian canines to carefully selected farmers in the mountainous regions in the north and center of the country. She and her colleagues have worked with 350 farmers throughout the wolves' range and placed nearly 700 pups with goat, sheep and cattle herds. She spends most of her time driving from village to village in the country's remote mountainous areas to visit the farmers and monitor how the guardian dogs are doing. Veterinary care and food are provided until the dogs reach adulthood. With dog after dog, she sees that the program is working, as farmers witness the canines' power against wolf attacks and gradually become more tolerant of wolves.

Estrela mountain dog Piloto waits for a cow in a mountain pasture in Central Portugal. Piloto wears a spiked leather collar, which once saved his life during a confrontation with wolves.

Farmer Alain Domini shows his organic sheep's milk cheese, which bears the image of a Great Pyrenees.

Great Pyrenees Mirabelle watches over a herd of Blackbelly "hair" sheep at Mathieu Mauriès's farm, Hogan des Vents, in southwest France.

Called "patou," the Great Pyrenees or Pyrenean mountain dog originated in the Pyrenees mountains on the border between France and Spain. The dog was first used to guard domestic animals from bears, wolves, foxes, lynxes and stray dogs. The French nobility adopted them as guard dogs in the Middle Ages.

When wolves were completely eliminated in France at the beginning of the 20th century, the Great Pyrenees, like guardian dogs elsewhere, lost their traditional guardian role. The breed almost became extinct, and the dogs survived only as companion animals.

Since 1992 wolves have gradually been returning, migrating from Italy to the southeast region of France. In 2019 the wolf population was about 530. With their return, predation on domestic animals has increased, even though the wolf's diet is primarily composed of wild prey such as mouflon and chamois.

To fight off wolves that approach livestock, French farmers are now once again turning to the Great Pyrenees for help.

Mathieu Mauriès with crossbred livestock guardian dog Onia on his farm, Hogan des Vents, in southwest France. The dogs are raised with the livestock from an early age and develop a special bond with the animals they protect.

MATHIEU AND THE PATOU FAMILY

In the heart of the Pyrenees mountains, about an hour away from the city of Toulouse, Mathieu Mauriès breeds and uses Great Pyrenees and Kangal dogs on his farm, Hogan des Vents. Mauriès had wanted to be a shepherd since childhood. In 2000 his goat herd was chased by neighbors' dogs. After this incident Mauriès decided to acquire his very first Great Pyrenees dog to help protect his animals. He fell in love with livestock guardian dogs and decided to select and breed them for other shepherds. Today he has 10 adult breeding dogs looking after a herd of about 180 sheep and a few goats. Three dogs would be sufficient to protect the herd, but genetics and selection require different lines of dogs to produce quality puppies. Mauriès also has 10 donkeys working with the dogs to protect the herd.

The puppies grow up in a rich environment in which they are introduced not only to the livestock they are meant to protect, but also to cats, chickens, cows and donkeys, a critical phase of their education. "When they become adults, they will be better able to manage complex situations," says Mauriès.

He spends time with the dogs to make sure they will be tolerant of people while doing their job as protectors. When they take on jobs as livestock protectors in the French mountains, the patous are likely to encounter hikers, mountain bikers and tourists who may not be familiar with agricultural practices and are afraid of guardian dogs because of their large size and loud bark. They do not realize the dogs are not aggressive but are just protecting the livestock. It is important to educate the public so that people understand the dogs' role in the mountains and know the attitude they should adopt if they encounter one. To this end a comic was produced to inform children and adults about the patous and how to behave in their presence, and it was later used in other countries, including Switzerland.

When Mauriès places the dogs with their new owners, he provides a detailed set of instructions to follow in the first months, acknowledging that while "the dogs know their job, people do not always know how to work with the dogs. My first teachers are my dogs."

DOGS VERSUS DOGS

Australia does not have wolves, but that doesn't mean livestock guardian dogs are out of work. They are employed to protect domestic animals against another kind of dog—the dingo. Dingoes are free-roaming dogs descended from canines brought to Australia by settlers thousands of years ago.

Researchers are now discovering that dingoes play an important ecological role. They help restore *biodiversity* in the environment by killing red foxes and cats, which are *introduced species*. This ultimately protects small native mammal species. However, dingoes are often hated by farmers because they go after livestock. To solve this problem, livestock guardian dogs such as Maremma sheepdogs have been used to keep dingoes away from farmers' animals, which, in turn, helps the dingoes perform their ecologically important role as the top dog in Australia.

A rescued dingo in Australia.

DOES USING LIVESTOCK GUARDIAN DOGS WORK?

Can a domestic animal truly help restore some of the world's wildest carnivores while at the same time saving livestock? Can it really scare away large predators such as grizzly bears and wolves? Studies have demonstrated the dogs' success, and many livestock owners report they have not lost any animals since the dogs arrived. In Portugal, deaths caused by wolves have been drastically reduced in three-quarters of the flocks protected by dogs. In North Dakota, dogs reduced coyote predation on sheep by 93 percent.

The presence of dogs with a herd does not always prevent wolves or other predators from attacking, but it can greatly reduce the number of livestock killed per attack, especially when several dogs are within the herd and working together to protect it.

People often wonder if particular breeds are better at protecting against a specific predator. In the United States, two researchers imported three European breeds that had not been used in the United States before—the Turkish Kangal, the Bulgarian Karakachan and the Portuguese cão de Gado Transmontano (also known as the Transmontano mastiff)—in order to conduct an experiment. These three breeds have a reputation for being bold toward predators but not aggressive toward humans and historically were used in areas with wolves or brown bears.

The researchers wanted to see if these breeds were better able to withstand conflicts with predators more powerful than coyotes—namely, wolves and grizzlies. They placed them with sheep herds in Idaho, Montana, Oregon, Washington and Wyoming in 2015 and 2016 and

Estrela mountain dogs Piloto and Fidalga work together to watch over shepherd Fernando da Silva Paiva's goat herd as the animals travel from the village where they spend the night to their daytime grazing pasture in Central Portugal.

compared their behavior to that of other guardian dogs commonly used in the United States. They also developed a test to examine the dogs' response when they encountered a wolf decoy on grazing land in the summer. They found there were few behavioral differences between the tested breeds, although the Kangals tended to be more investigative when engaging a decoy and the Karakachans more vigilant. The Transmontanos were more capable of distinguishing between a threatening wolf decoy and a nonthreatening deer decoy. These results may help farmers make more educated decisions in choosing the right breed of dog for their specific situation.

Even though having guardian dogs is recognized as one of the best ways to protect livestock against predators, negative perceptions continue, and to some sheep and cattle owners, saying yes to using dogs to protect their livestock means saying yes to the presence of wild predators. The Trump administration in the United States proposed removing legal protections for gray wolves and grizzlies, a troubling move since these animals occupy only a fraction of their historical habitat. A study of the status and ecological effects of the world's largest carnivores, published in 2014, shows that predators such as wolves, cougars and lions are necessary to maintain biodiversity and that their habitats should be preserved or restored. In the United States, wolves are poached every year by trophy hunters and ranchers. The deaths are often unreported, and therefore it is difficult to track how many wolves are killed. Scientists can sometimes estimate the losses indirectly. In Wisconsin, for example, more than half of all radio-collared wolves between 1979 and 2012 disappeared, presumably due to hunting. (Radio collars are placed on wolves to monitor population numbers.)

Kangal shepherd Oroul with a herd of donkeys on Mathieu Mauriès's farm. The donkeys work with the dogs to protect livestock against predators. Because of their height, the donkeys can spot an approaching predator before the dogs do.

In Namibia, Armas Shaanika, Cheetah Conservation Fund's chief goat herder, is regarded as the "Livestock Guarding Dog Whisperer." He understands how the dogs work with the livestock. He has helped raise almost all of CCF's puppies for the past 20 years, including Kangal shepherd Spots.

DOG ON DUTY: PROTECTING TOGETHER

Most of the time, guardian dogs are excellent at their jobs as protectors—they have been doing it for thousands of years. However, in order to be fully successful they need a bit of help from their human friends. Fighting off powerful predators is a big task, and dogs, as good as they are, cannot always do it all alone. Shepherds and ranchers can help their four-legged partners by adding fences to keep their sheep or cattle safe, moving animals indoors at night and adapting their farming practices.

Fencing helps control livestock movement and dispersal, making it easier for the dogs to protect the animals and allowing them to focus on the area they need to defend. Shepherds can keep vulnerable animals such as newborns, the young or injured, and pregnant females, indoors. They can also time lambing or calving to occur in specific periods rather than throughout the entire year. They can confine livestock in bad weather, when predators tend to come closer to the herd, and avoid pastures near areas with forest or dense vegetation, which allow predators to approach easily without being seen.

Shepherds must also be sure they have enough dogs to protect their herds. Many factors influence the risk of predation, such as how many predators there are in an area, how vulnerable the livestock is, the type of habitat, the size of the herd and the farm's management practices. One dog may be enough to protect smaller herds that are kept indoors at night and graze in areas with fewer predators and more wild prey, but it is preferable to have at least two dogs per herd since they work best as a team and are better able to face predators to protect themselves and the herd.

A wildlife officer demonstrates the Washington Department of Fish and Wildlife's Karelian Bear Dog Program during a public event at Woodland Park Zoo in Seattle. The dog is investigating a person dressed up as a bear near a garbage bin.

WILDLIFE GUARDIANS

While guardian dogs have traditionally worked at protecting people's livestock against predator attacks, their role has expanded to include helping wild species stay out of trouble and protecting wild animals that cannot defend themselves against more powerful predators.

SCARING BEARS AWAY TO PROTECT THEM

In North America bears sometimes get into trouble by coming close to where humans live, visiting backyards or campsites to look for food. In the past wildlife officers usually dealt with the situation by killing the problem bear or relocating it to another area. Most of the time, however, relocation does not work. Many bears find their way back, and those that don't try to return sometimes have trouble finding food in their new environment and do not survive. In the early 2000s, dogs were called upon to help with this difficult conservation problem.

Wind River Bear Institute's founder, Carrie Hunt, works with her lead Karelian bear dog, Akela, and a taxidermied grizzly bear. The bear mount was donated to the Institute from Montana Fish, Wildlife and Parks for public education and puppy testing.

The Karelian bear dog, originally from northeastern Europe, is known to be fearless and capable of standing up to large mammals such as bears. Early records show that ancestors of Karelian bear dogs lived alongside Vikings in Scandinavia and were even buried with their masters.

Over the centuries people used Karelian bear dogs to hunt big animals in regions that today are part of Russia and Finland.

In the United States, Carrie Hunt, a biologist in Montana, wanted to reduce conflict between people and bears. She discovered that Karelian bear dogs could help achieve this goal. She imported her first dogs from Finland in the 1990s and created an organization in 1996 called the Wind River Bear Institute, which trains Karelian bear dogs to save bears' lives by chasing them away.

You may wonder how a dog is able to do that when it is a fraction of the bear's size. But because the bear is not used to being confronted by a barking dog, in most cases it will choose to run away. Karelian bear dogs are especially helpful when bears are visiting particular spots, such as a garbage dump they associate with food.

A wildlife officer traps the bear at the site and then brings in a team of two dogs, who bark at the animal to let it know it should never come back to this location. Usually the bear gets the message and finds another place to hunt. For this approach to really work, however, the thing that attracted the bear in the first place also needs to be addressed. In the case of a garbage dump, for example, an electric fence could be built around the dump, or bear-proof containers could be installed.

Karelian puppies at the Wind River Bear Institute go through rigorous training. When they are two months old, they undergo a series of tests over two weeks to determine the path they will take. Trainers want to find out what pups are best suited to the job, since dogs from the same litter do not all possess the same capabilities. Just 20 percent of a litter will be able to successfully work with bears.

Karelian bear dog puppy Traveler poses in front of a taxidermied grizzly bear after completing his bear test.

Karelian bear dog puppy Hayduke approaches a black-bear carcass for the first time as part of his bear test. The black bear was donated to the Wind River Bear Institute by Montana Fish, Wildlife and Parks for puppy testing. Hayduke's ears and tail are up as he approaches the bear cautiously but with the confidence characteristic of a "bear conflict" level Karelian bear dog.

Karelian bear dog Traveler poses with a black-bear carcass after completing his test.

The first test involves crawling through a confined area, something working bear dogs must do frequently to chase bears out from under people's houses or track them in their *dens*. In the second test, trainers lead puppies to an upright metal barrel to see how they react to the presence of something large and imposing. The puppies are also presented with carcasses of smaller animals such as deer. During these tests the trainers teach the puppies the right behaviors and also evaluate personality, boldness, level of motivation and, ultimately, how they react in a frightening situation that involves bears. In the very last test, puppies must face stuffed bears and cougars placed in the field. These props come from animals that were killed as a result of conflicts with people. Hunt and her team carefully observe how each pup approaches the situation.

"Good with the bear," Hunt says of the ones that pass the test. When the top dogs, the strongest and the bravest, move on to work with real bears, they are expected to perform a job where the wrong move or the slightest hesitation can lead to serious injury. This is why it is so important to select the right dogs for the job.

Karelian bear dogs are deployed in various parts of North America, from Alaska, where they locate polar bear dens, to Alberta, Washington and Nevada. As polar bears move closer to human activity because of climate change and melting sea ice, Karelian bear dogs are expected to play a greater role in keeping the bears safe and away from people.

Of course, people also have to do their part to reduce bear-human conflict. For example, people who live in bear country must always be sure to lock up garbage and food in bear-resistant containers.

ENCOURAGING SOCIAL DISTANCING

In the United States and Canada, dogs have been used to help manage wildlife that comes too close to humans, particularly in national parks, where the high number of visitors often results in human-wildlife conflicts. In 2016 Glacier National Park hired Gracie the Bark Ranger to keep park visitors and wildlife a safe distance apart. Gracie is a border collie who works hard to shepherd bighorn sheep and mountain goats out of areas where there are lots of people. In the winter Gracie moves deer out of the park's residential area to reduce the presence of mountain lions, who are attracted to the deer. Gracie was trained at the Wind River Bear Institute, but she doesn't work with bears or other predators. Another part of her job description is to act as a wildlife safety ambassador along with the park ranger, reminding people to stay a safe distance away from all wildlife. When on duty, Gracie wears an orange vest indicating that she is a wildlife working dog.

A member of the Washington Department of Fish and Wildlife's Karelian Bear Dog Program, dressed up as a bear, demonstrates how bears can be attracted to unsecured garbage bins. The event at Woodland Park Zoo in Seattle was aimed at educating the public on how to reduce bear–human conflicts.

Border collie Gracie the Bark Ranger works at Glacier National Park in Montana. NATIONAL PARK SERVICE/ALICE W. BIEL

Maremma sheepdogs Tula (front) and Mezzo (back) are protecting little penguins from foxes. Tula, now retired, is teaching Mezzo the ropes to take over as the lead guardian dog.

THE PENGUIN PROTECTORS

The Maremma and Abruzzeses sheepdogs are from the Abruzzo region of central Italy's Apennine Mountains and the adjacent Maremma plains. They work with shepherds during the day and stay in enclosures with the sheep at night. In the winter the dogs and sheep spend their time on the lower plains, and at the start of the summer the shepherds travel for several days to take the animals to the cooler pastures of the Apennine Mountains. There the Maremmas guard livestock from wolves and bears. The dogs are patient and gentle with their sheep and familiar people, but are vigilant against intruders. They become active and noisy if their herd is under threat.

In the 1980s Australia imported Maremma sheep-dogs from Italy, and since then they have become the most widely used livestock guardian dog in the country. Livestock producers use them to protect their domestic animals from predators such as dingoes, and in some regions the dogs serve as wildlife guardians.

Middle Island is a small island connected by a tidal sand bridge to the city of Warrnambool in southwestern Australia. For decades the island has been home to a colony of little penguins, the smallest species of penguin in the world. It also provides habitat and nesting locations for a number of other seabirds, including short-tailed shearwaters. But when foxes discovered they could reach the island at low tide, they nearly wiped out the penguin colony. By 2005 the population had gone from 504 penguins arriving in one evening to less than 10. That year 268 carcasses were found in a single day.

Australia has a long history of invasive species decimating native wildlife. Early settlers introduced red foxes to the country for the purpose of sport hunting. The foxes adapted to their environment and began to devour *native species*. The flightless little penguins were easy prey.

A local chicken farmer, Allan "Swampy" Marsh, had trained Maremma sheepdogs to protect his free-range chickens from foxes. When he heard what was happening to the little penguins, he suggested applying the same tactic. How did the unlikely animal-kingdom alliance between four-legged-guardians and penguins come about? In 2006 local officials agreed to deploy the first Maremma dog, Oddball, to Middle Island to protect the penguins from foxes during the birds' breeding season, between October and February. Oddball had spent her whole life

Little penguins are the smallest species of penguin in the world.

Middle Island, a small island connected by a tidal sand bridge to the city of Warrnambool in Australia, is home to a colony of little penguins.

guarding Marsh's free-range chickens, so she figured out what to do. She was introduced to the penguins' distinct smell and came to recognize them as members of her *pack*. She treated the penguins like any other type of livestock to be protected.

Having a canine bodyguard on Middle Island was a huge success—no penguins were attacked by foxes on Oddball's watch. The program, run by the Middle Island Project Working Group, continued, and two other Maremma guardian dogs, Eudy and Tula, took over Oddball's job. During the penguins' breeding season, the dogs stayed on the island for several days in a row, with a supply of food and water, watching over the penguins from a raised walkway. On their days off, the amazing canine bodyguards returned to Warrnambool, where they interacted with visitors and helped educate people about wildlife conservation. Middle Island is closed to the public to protect penguin burrows from human trampling, but every summer people who want to learn more about the project can book a "Meet the Maremma" tour to learn about the penguin protectors. Between 2006 and 2017, the penguin population rose from 4 to 182.

Unfortunately, in 2017 foxes attacked Middle Island and killed 142 penguins. The penguins are only on the island during breeding season, but that year the penguins had arrived earlier than usual, in June. The dogs are not present on the island between March and September, as there are normally no penguins in the wintertime, and the sea is rough and the crossing dangerous. Since then measures have been taken to better protect the penguins. The dogs are now deployed to the island in June, and penguin numbers are on the rise again, thanks to the hard work of their canine protectors. In 2020 the population was estimated to be between 70 and 100 penguins.

Tula retired in 2019, and Eudy is helping train two new dogs, Mezzo and Isola, who have joined the penguin protecting pack. While popular for their work with penguins, Maremmas are now also protecting other wildlife, such as the endangered eastern barred bandicoot, a small marsupial found near Hamilton, Victoria.

Maremma sheepdog Mezzo is now Middle Island's lead guardian dog. Mezzo ("middle" in Italian) works on the island in partnership with another dog named Isola ("island" in Italian).

Wirehaired Jack Russell terrier Casey poses in front of the Center for Conservation Biology's Conservation Canines program at the University of Washington. Casey works as an ambassador for the program, visiting classrooms and participating at speaking events.

3

A NOSE FOR CONSERVATION

Knowing where different species live, the kind of habitat they need to survive and how individuals move and use the landscape is vital to conservation efforts. All over the world, dogs are increasingly putting their noses to work with ecologists, conservation biologists and wildlife managers to help them collect information that helps us understand and protect wildlife and wild areas. Where do these amazing dogs come from, and how do they become super sniffers?

GRADUATION DAY

It is an unusually hot day in May in downtown Indianapolis, Indiana. Everyone is getting ready for an extraordinary graduation ceremony on the lawn of the Indiana state capitol building. The graduating class has seven participants, who traveled from four different states—Virginia, Kansas, Utah and Oregon—to enroll in an intensive nine-week program that began in February.

People walking on the streets of downtown Indianapolis stop to take a closer look at this unusual ceremony. All graduates have shiny coats and a good level of energy, despite the heat.

Glenn Cramer and K9 Waylon

Certificate of Training

for satisfactory completion of a 400 hour Wildlife Law
Enforcement K9 Tracking and Detection School.

Awarded this 14 day of May 2019

German shorthaired pointer Waylon poses with his graduation certificate after satisfactorily completing 400 hours of training at the Canine Resource Protection program. K9 Waylon now works for the Virginia Department of Wildlife Resources' Conservation Police.

The hardworking students about to be celebrated today for their achievements are canines, mostly Labrador retrievers. They are the brand-new graduates of the 2019 *K9* Major Memorial School. The name of the school changes each year to honor a different working dog who has died. Major was the most recent, having retired and passed away at age 12. This canine training program, called the Canine Resource Protection Program, has been run every year since 1997 by Jeffrey Milner, a conservation officer and coordinator of the K9 unit in the Indiana Department of Natural Resources.

At K9 school, the dogs and their human partners—conservation officers employed by state natural resources departments across the United States—learn to track people, locate firearms and detect wildlife in all conditions, from mud and rain to snow. Once they are back home, the new graduates help search areas, retrieve evidence, detect different wildlife species and find people who poach plants and animals. As of 2020, 30 states had an official K9 program within their natural resources department, and Milner has trained over 70 dog teams so far.

Each state has specific wildlife issues that canines can assist with. In Indiana, for example, the program employs 12 dogs, half of them adopted from shelters. All the dogs are trained to help Indiana fight the illegal harvesting of ginseng, a plant that is often shipped overseas. In the past, officers had a hard time finding and arresting the people who were stealing the plants because the poachers hid their digging tools and the plants they had collected deep in the woods where nobody could find them. But the dogs could easily track the poachers and quickly locate the evidence officers could not find on their own. "Ginseng arrests are up dramatically since we have the dogs," Milner says.

Today he proudly places a police badge on each of the seven graduating dogs. They are now official police dogs and ready to go to work!

The badge K9-24 belongs to Indiana conservation officer K9 Marley, who became an officer in the 2016 Indiana Canine Resource Protection Program.

Indiana conservation officer Jeffrey Milner poses with yellow Labrador retriever K9 Fury. Fury was rescued from an animal shelter in 2011. He retired in July 2020 after working in wildlife law enforcement in Indiana and now resides with Milner and his family.

Australian cattle dog Max is a rescue who first worked for the Conservation Canines program before joining Rogue Detection Teams. Max and all other canines in the program are trained first on wolverine scat. Because wolverines are so elusive and rare, researchers are always interested in the dogs' ability to locate their poop.

A NOSE FOR DATA

When it comes to helping scientists collect information about plants and animals, detection dogs are quick and efficient. Because their expert noses can smell what humans can't, dogs are sent to find tiny elusive or rare endangered animals and plants in huge areas. They also detect unwanted and harmful species, find animal traces such as minuscule scat (the polite word for poop) or caterpillar larvae that are almost invisible to the human eye, and retrieve animal carcasses by following scents hidden in deep vegetation or even in the water. They move easily in rough terrain and do their job with unlimited energy, focus, physical strength and agility. They are always willing to work with a human partner and are eager to please.

Some of the other wildlife-detection methods, including camera trapping, darting and collaring, tracking plates (plates covered with a material that critters leave tracks on when they walk over it) and hair snares (devices that collect hair from an animal) can be invasive, create disturbance or introduce bias to the research. For example, a researcher may use *bait* to draw an animal to a location with a camera, hair snare or track plate. This may mean that only dominant or very inquisitive animals approach. As a result the researcher may not gain a full understanding of how a species is using a landscape. In contrast, detection dogs who sniff for the droppings of these same species are not choosing between males or females or dominant or subordinate animals. They are finding the poop where the animal actually prefers to eat, sleep and otherwise use its territory, so the data they help collect is not biased.

The collaring method provides researchers with detailed information, but in order to place a collar on an animal, researchers have to catch it, which creates a lot of stress. Once the collar is on, it can be heavy and disorienting. In some cases it may disrupt feeding and resting habits or cause injuries from rubbing or being too tight.

Dogs can be trained to sniff out just about anything, and our imagination is perhaps the only limit when it comes to potential tasks for these extraordinary canines.

Casey is the most mischievous pack member of the University of Washington's Conservation Canines program. After several months of training, Casey was deployed to San Diego to help researchers locate the Pacific pocket mouse. This species was thought to be extinct but was later rediscovered, and canines such as Casey were called in to conduct noninvasive surveys that helped determine the population and habitat range of this tiny, elusive mammal.

However, successful working conservation dogs must have more than just a good nose. They must be physically fit, able to tolerate heat and cold and have sufficient stamina to search for hours in rugged and often inhospitable conditions. A dog without the drive to want to search every day and play ball will not do well, no matter how fit it is. Most of all, in the same way a livestock guardian dog cannot do all the work on its own, a conservation detection dog must work as a team with a two-legged partner.

Max and Rogue Detection Teams cofounder Jennifer Hartman had many adventures together, such as collecting data on northern spotted owls in California, fishers in Oregon, wolf and caribou in Alberta, and lynx in Washington. Max even traveled all the way to Cambodia to assist in tiger and leopard surveys. "I could not ask for a more sweet-tempered, big-hearted, mischievous, brilliant detection dog," Hartman says.

LAST CHANCE FOR UNWANTED CANINES

Even though their job is important, super sniffer dogs do not start out as anything special. Unlike some of the specialized livestock guardian dogs, conservation dogs do not need to be a specific breed. In fact, organizations such as Conservation Canines, Working Dogs for Conservation, Rogue Detection Teams and Detection Dogs for Conservation find their best dogs in animal shelters.

Animals chosen to be conservation dogs are often the misfits of the dog world. They are often highly energetic, athletic, always willing to play and in need of lots of exercise. While most dogs love toys, these ones have an obsessive play drive and refuse to put down their toy no matter what. In a home where their needs are not met, they can become aggressive and destructive. These high-energy canines who never quit are not good family pets, and

Conservation dogs have unlimited energy, need lots of exercise and are obsessed with playing ball. They do not make good pets and were often surrendered by their owners to animal shelters before being adopted by conservation programs.

Unwanted shelter dogs get a chance to redirect their insatiable play drive to wildlife search missions.

Pips and Heath Smith are on a mission to find the droppings of the elusive Haida Gwaii ermine in the forest.

they often are taken to shelters because their owners just cannot handle them.

Sadly, once in shelters they have little hope of being adopted. They end up being euthanized or living out their lives in the shelter. Yet many unwanted canines may make ideal conservation dogs. Their intense energy, obsession with play and ability to focus are perfect traits for working in the field with handlers for long periods of time.

Of course, not every shelter dog is cut out for conservation work. The organizations that recruit dogs from shelters evaluate candidates by putting them through a series of exercises. The goal is to see whether the dog has the drive required to be trained to take on conservation assignments in the field.

The US-based organization Working Dogs for Conservation has partnered with the International Fund for Animal Welfare to identify suitable dogs and connect them with working-dog groups that can place them in successful careers on the front lines of wildlife conservation. Through their Rescues 2the Rescue program, started in 2015, they have created online tools to teach shelter staff around the world how to recognize canine candidates.

RESCUING CANINE MISFITS

Heath Smith has worked with Conservation Canines for over 20 years and is the cofounder of Rogue Detection Teams in the United States. Nicknamed the Dogfather by his team (or pack!) of dog handlers, Smith actually describes himself as a cat person. He never had a dog growing up, but when he met his first detection dog, Gator, an Australian cattle dog, it changed his life forever.

"He taught me a different language," he says. Today Smith takes pride in giving dogs a second chance at life. "We are trying to find those dogs that are out of options," he says. Over the years Smith has facilitated the rescue of over 40 energetic, unwanted dogs from shelters to redirect their insatiable play drive to wildlife search missions. "They don't have any hope of getting adopted, but with us these misfits become heroes," he says. Working on projects in the field, the dogs gain a new sense of purpose. "Often when dogs join our team we can see that they can be hesitant to partake in certain behaviors, like tugging on a ball or even just roaming a bit further from us. So we work to let them be themselves. We want them to be independent, confident and trust us."

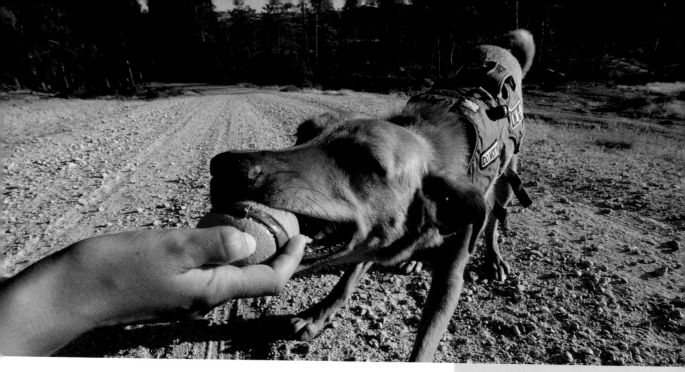

Rogue Detection Teams pack member Hera is rewarded with a ball game after detecting wolf poop in Portugal.

LEARNING TO BE A CONSERVATION CANINE

BALL OBSESSION

Once a dog is rescued from the shelter, the handler starts the process of teaching the canine its new job, which builds on its obsession with a ball. The ball is used as a reward for finding the object of a search. The dog learns to identify different target odors and ultimately comes to associate finding the target with getting the reward: the handler throws the ball immediately after the dog finds the target. In this way the dog learns to seek the target persistently in order to keep earning the reward.

The dog is so motivated to get the ball reward that it will not stop looking for the target until it is found, even if it is hidden in the most obscure or inaccessible locations— deep vegetation, mud or even water. Nothing will distract the dog from the mission. "What is fantastic about the dogs is that they don't care about anything else but getting their ball. If the scat is floating in the water or up on a

Adopted from a rescue shelter in California, chocolate Labrador Diesel now works for Alberta Environment and Parks' Conservation K-9 Program, detecting invasive mussels.

German shepherd Seuss alerts his human partner after finding an invasive-mussel training sample on the shore of Upper Kananaskis Lake, AB.

volcanic rock, the dogs work their best to either reach it or point it out to their handlers," says Heath Smith of Rogue Detection Teams.

Detection dogs can be trained on any object that has an odor, which is almost everything, and they learn to pick up different odors very quickly—scat, ivory, rhino horns, shark fins, bushmeat, even firearms and ammunition. Scooby, one of the Rogue Detection Teams dogs, is able to recognize well over 30 different scents. There is virtually no limit to what the canines can find, and with an experienced dog handler, a new canine recruit can get to work quickly, often in just a few days.

Of course, dogs that come from shelters may have a few challenges at first. For example, some of the rescued animals have never been outside and may initially be afraid of going into the woods with the handler, so it can take a little more time, patience and love to figure out how to teach the dog that it can actually be very exciting to be out in the woods and get one's paws wet!

THE LOOK

A good conservation dog must be an excellent communicator. Once it has located the target, it must let its handler know, without interacting with or compromising the find in any way. Referred to as an *alert*, this notification typically takes the form of sitting or lying down near the target. But dogs have different ways of signaling a discovery to the handler, whether it is a crouch, a look, a sit or a lie-down. Most of all it is about the look, as once the dog has locked eyes with its handler, the human knows right away that the canine partner is onto something. The process is all about communication and trust.

THE SEARCH

In conservation jobs, a dog usually performs three types of searches: air scenting, in which the dog raises its nose, sniffing to catch scent on the wind; tracking, where the dog keeps its nose low to the ground, following the scent and direction of the target; and trailing, in which the dog uses a combination of air-scenting and tracking techniques. Air scenting is the most common detection technique used in conservation.

The dogs at Rogue Detection Teams, for example, are taught air scenting more than tracking because they primarily look for scat (a nonmoving target!) rather than people on the move. This organization will consider all types of dogs but finds that some breeds, such as Labrador retrievers, German shepherds, border collies and Australian cattle dogs, are more naturally suited to air scenting. Dogs such as bloodhounds can do well in air-scenting work but most excel at ground tracking, such as following the trail of wildlife poachers on the move. "I don't spend a lot of time judging the dogs by breed," Smith says. "It really comes down to each individual in a lot of cases." Smith acknowledges, however, that some breeds could be too small while others are too large, such as a Great Dane.

No matter what they do and how they do it, no job is too big for these eager canines, who can happily work for many years. Some of the long-term four-legged employees with Conservation Canines and Rogue Detection Teams are well over 10 years old, but they do not seem to want to quit. They are still active every day and love to play in the field. When they are finally ready for retirement, they will have a comfortable couch waiting for them. They are usually adopted by their handlers, who want to keep their working dogs for life.

Seuss methodically searches for minuscule, well-camouflaged zebra mussels along the shoreline of Upper Kananaskis Lake, AB.

A researcher monitors a little brown bat, a species that has been severely hit by the deadly white-nose syndrome in eastern North America.

DOG ON DUTY: BAT DETECTOR

White-nose syndrome (WNS) is a deadly fungus that has killed millions of bats in eastern Canada and the United States since it was discovered in 2006. WNS has been described as the most catastrophic wildlife disease to hit North America in recorded history and is now spreading west.

The deadly disease has not arrived in southeast Alaska yet, but scientists in the Alaska Department of Fish and Game are monitoring bat populations closely, particularly the little brown bats that have already been decimated by WNS on the east coast of North America.

Because the fungus attacks the small mammals during hibernation, it is important for the scientists to find the bats' hibernacula—the nooks and crannies in which the animals hibernate through the winter. However, it's difficult to locate the small holes in rocky outcrops and under tree roots that serve as hibernacula in Alaska's forests. Scientists radio-tagged and tracked bats from airplanes to try to locate the animals' hibernacula. As long as the bats did not go too deep into the holes, the researchers could hear the signal from the air. Most bats went deeper, however, which is why scientists found only 10 sites over four years of radio-tracking.

In the summer of 2019, Jack, a canine working for Rogue Detection Teams, and handler Collette Yee came to help. Jack was trained on the scent of bat guano and fur, then sent out to look for hibernacula in the Juneau area. Bats visit hibernacula during the summer to locate suitable places to hibernate and also to mate. They circle in front of a site, land near the entrance and crawl into the hibernaculum to mate. When they land and crawl, they leave a scent behind that Jack can detect. In just one month he found five new hibernation spots. This information will help scientists be better prepared to protect bats from WNS in the future.

Cindy Sawchuk, of Alberta Environment and Parks' Aquatic Invasive Species Program, and her work partner, black Lab/golden retriever cross Hilo.

A UNIQUE BOND

TEAMWORK FOR CONSERVATION

Dogs are smelling machines. They can track a smell almost nonstop and can determine the general direction a scent is coming from, a huge advantage when they are searching unknown environments. However, a dog's ability to detect an odor successfully can be affected by a variety of factors, such as wind and vegetation.

This is where the handler comes in. The two-legged partner must know how to work with the dog and help unleash its true sniffing power. While the canine's job is solely to smell, the handler pays attention to changes in the environment and considers things such as wind speed and direction, how the odor moves and how the terrain and air temperature affect it. The handler also has to understand the habits of the species being sought in order

Nose to the ground, Hilo sniffs for a hidden tiny zebra mussel on the shore of Upper Kananaskis Lake, AB.

to help focus and lead surveys on the ground and maximize the chances of locating the target.

Usually a detection dog moves in a zigzag pattern toward the source of an odor. The pattern takes the shape of a cone, with the source of the odor at the "point" of the cone. As the dog approaches the source, the odor becomes fresher and more concentrated. A strong gust of wind can help the scent cone become more narrow, and the dog can almost run straight to the source of the odor.

Of course, an odor does not always cooperate. Its intensity may rise or fall with changing humidity, temperature and air currents, or it can stay in vegetation or under logs and other objects. When physical obstacles or air currents shift the scent away from the source, a dog can lose track of it. For example, a canine looking for the scat of a species may identify the general location of an odor but be unable to pinpoint its exact source because it's on the other side of a hill, which creates a gap in the odor. In this case it is the handler's job to figure out where the odor is coming from and help the dog relocate the lost scent by moving the dog over the hill. What truly creates success is the teamwork between the handler and the dog, the unique bond and trust that develop between them.

Every time a dog is assigned to a new project, researchers must be educated about what conservation canines can and cannot do. "A lot of studies are designed for human surveyors, and the researchers want to put the dogs into that formula," Heath Smith says. "They think of a dog as a superhuman who is going to detect everything." But each situation has those variables like wind direction that affect the dog's ability to perform the job. "It is a different world for the dog."

Conservation dogs often get to travel the world and work in different environments. But that doesn't mean their fieldwork is a walk in the park. Because the dogs are generally hired to locate rare species, they may become distracted and bored when they don't find anything. Sometimes it takes days or weeks of searching a large area to find a species' scat. If the dog finds only a few droppings (and hence receives few rewards and opportunities to play ball), its motivation can decrease rapidly. If this happens, the handler must keep the dog engaged and focused by doing such things as hiding training samples of the target for the dog to find so that there are opportunities for reward. On the other hand, when there is a lot of poop to find, the dog may never want to stop, and the handler must be careful not to wear out the eager four-legged partner. Detection dogs focus intensely on their missions, and it is always the responsibility of their human partners to make their jobs easier and keep them safe from whatever danger they could encounter in the field—sharp objects, dangerous animals and so on. The welfare of the dogs comes first.

Jennifer Hartman gently hands Max a ball, the reward he was waiting for. "The way he played with the ball was so wild," Hartman says. "His eyes would go cross-eyed, and he would just stare at the ball until I handed it to him. Then he would roll on it and bounce it off of his pointy snout."

Julianne Ubigau and her work partner, Casey, from the University of Washington's Conservation Canines program.

TRAINING THE TWO-LEGGED PARTNER

While the dogs catch on to their jobs relatively quickly, the people involved with the canines often require more training. It usually takes about two years to train handlers in an organization such as Rogue Detection Teams, as they need to gain the knowledge and experience required to read a dog's signs and develop the patience to work with such a high-energy animal. Handlers have to learn to think like a dog, speak like a dog and be intuitive and flexible. Because every dog is different, there is no textbook to tell a handler how to interact with a particular dog.

"They must be able to take all the pieces of a puzzle and complete it without really knowing what the puzzle is. In the same way we are looking for dogs that can problem-solve, be independent and think for themselves, we teach the handlers to be the same way, so they become a team," says Smith.

The handler must always be careful when communicating with the dog and should not reward it when it finds something that is not the target scent, as this would compromise the dog's ability to be successful. And while dog handlers have to pay attention to what the dogs say to them in the field, they also need to watch themselves and consider what they say to the dog and how they say it. The human partner's own emotions and attitude in the field can greatly influence the dog, who is always looking to its two-legged friend for signals and changes in behaviors.

NOT A JOB FOR EVERYONE

Not everybody can be a dog handler. "Handling a dog is vastly different from training a dog," says Luke Edwards, a dog trainer and handler with Canidae Development, a group in Australia that conducts environmental surveys with dogs. "I have trained several handlers and the thing that makes a good handler is their ability to form a bond with their dogs."

Being a dog handler is more than a job. It is a lifestyle that requires a great deal of commitment and passion. The handlers live with the dogs 24 hours a day, travel all over the world, move from one study site to another and work with different dogs at each location. They can be away from home on a field study with their canine partner for a few days or a few months, and in some cases they live in tents in remote wilderness areas. Conservation detection dogs often work long hours in conditions that may be harsh, facing extreme cold or heat, snow or rain. Handlers always stay close to their dogs in the field, walking through the same terrain as their more agile canine partners. They must keep physically fit and maintain a positive attitude.

Kalo is a Malinois born in Slovakia who started his job as a detection dog with Conservation Lower Zambezi in 2020. He is full of energy and loves to work for his ball and his primary handler, Wildlife Ranger Peter Tembo. MICHAEL HENSMAN (INVICTUS K9 & CONSERVATION LOWER ZAMBEZI)

Rita Santos and Hera in Parque Natural do Alvão in Central Portugal.

RITA AND HERA

At age 14, Rita Santos was spending more time at the local dog shelter than at school in her home city of Lisbon, Portugal. Santos loved animals and volunteered every day to look after abandoned dogs, cleaning their kennels, feeding them, taking them for walks and giving them medication. Spending quality time with the dogs at the shelter helped the teenager get through a difficult time in her life, when she felt lonely and out of place in a new high school she did not like. The dogs helped Santos as much as she helped them. Sometimes she just sat with the dogs and watched them play. Every time she took a dog out of a kennel to go for a walk, she noticed its "smile" and how happy it was to enjoy a moment outside.

Over time Santos developed a real expertise in training dogs, and then one day she met Heath Smith, who had come to the shelter where she worked. He was in Portugal looking for dogs to support a new wolf study in partnership with

Conservation Canines in the United States and the nonprofit group Grupo Lobo in Portugal.

At the shelter Smith became interested in a dog named Zeus, and he asked Santos for help. This marked the start of a new career for her as a conservation dog handler. She was just finishing high school in 2013 when she began an eight-month stint surveying areas in Central Portugal with the dog, looking for wolf poop. The objective of the study was to find out whether the Douro River was a natural barrier for wolves in the Portuguese landscape. If wolves are able to cross the river, they can expand their territories, find more wild prey and breed with animals south of the river, which improves genetic diversity.

Raised in Lisbon, a big city, Santos initially had a hard time working in the field, following the dog in the woods and learning about local wildlife. But she loves the job!

In 2017 Santos adopted Hera, a two-year-old street dog. Hera had been rescued as a puppy and placed in a shelter. She was adopted when she was six months old, but a few weeks later the new owners returned her because she was too much to handle. Hera had lots of energy and had destroyed everything in the house. She stayed at the shelter until Santos finally discovered her. Santos needed a new conservation detection dog, and Hera was the perfect match.

At first Hera was shy and uncomfortable around people, but she had a lot of potential. "As soon as you took the ball out, she did not care about the world anymore. She was really focused," Santos remembers. The pair is now a winning team, working for wildlife conservation groups across Europe. They have been on many adventures together, from searching for turtle nests in the South of France to looking for brown bears in the Pyrenees to combing the Crau plain of southeastern France to find a rare, tiny species of cricket that camouflages itself well and moves quickly in the environment. "She was just a machine, covering every centimeter of the place, being really fast and really good!"

Hera alerts her handler after discovering wolf scat in Parque Natural do Alvão in Central Portugal.

Alberta Environment and Parks'
Cindy Sawchuk and canine partner
Hilo survey the shoreline of
Upper Kananaskis Lake, AB.

4

TOP DOGS SAVING THE WILD

Whether their noses are detecting scat, invasive species, poison or illegal wildlife products, conservation dogs are helping humans address some of the most pressing environmental issues our planet faces and making a difference for endangered wildlife around the world.

SEARCHING FOR THE NEVER-SEEN ERMINE

Heath Smith and his canine partner, an Australian cattle dog named Pips, traveled a long way from Washington State to help out Berry Wijdeven, the species-at-risk recovery coordinator for the British Columbia Ministry of Forests, Lands, Natural Resource Operations and Rural Development. They met up in Haida Gwaii, a remote group of islands located about 80 kilometers (50 miles) off the northern coast of British Columbia.

Wijdeven was anxiously waiting for Smith and Pips to arrive to help him solve a problem. He had spent nine years looking for a subspecies of ermine found only in Haida Gwaii. Sightings of the ermine, which is designated as threatened, are rare, making it difficult to determine much about the population's diet, health and use of habitat. Wijdeven has seen 14 dead

Heath Smith and Berry Wijdeven closely examine an ermine scat Pips discovered in the forest of Haida Gwaii, BC.

ermine in his career, mostly as bycatch in marten traps but some also killed by cats, and he hears about three to five sightings a year from other people who have encountered them. He had tried every single method he could think of to locate ermines in the forests of Haida Gwaii— track plates, live traps, hair snares, den boxes (boxes with a small opening, which animals will use as dens, leaving behind evidence in the form of hair or scat), automatic camera stations—but nothing had worked. Only two ermines had been captured in more than 6,700 trap nights between 1992 and 1997. After all those years of hard work, some biologists researching the ermine, Wijdeven included, had seen dead ermines but never a live one.

When nothing is known about a species, it becomes difficult to protect it adequately. This was why Wijdeven reached out to Smith and the Conservation Canines program for help. Pips's mission was to locate the scat that ermines leave behind in the forest. First he had to become familiar with its scent. Because Haida Gwaii ermines are so rare, it was not possible to get the relevant samples needed to teach the dog how to recognize the smell. So for this assignment, Pips was trained on the droppings of a different ermine species that lives off-island.

Once Pips understood his mission, he worked tirelessly in the forest to find ermine poop, walking alongside creeks, examining logs from end to end, sniffing under woody debris. For 16 days Wijdeven and Smith followed Pips. They hiked 40 to 50 kilometers (25 to 31 miles) and took the dog to 25 different sites in hopes of finding droppings the size of macaroni tubes.

One might think it would be easier for a dog to find a needle in a haystack than ermine droppings. But Pips succeeded! By the end of the project, he had managed

Pips makes eye contact with his human partner to indicate that he has found the target—Haida Gwaii ermine droppings the size of macaroni tubes.

Conservation canines like Pips are happy to work all day, walking over rocks and alongside creeks, climbing logs and trekking through rough terrain, in expectation of a reward—playing with their ball—after successfully locating wildlife scat.

Conservation dogs have been used to detect a variety of species, including black bears.

to find 11 samples. Although Wijdeven had hoped for a higher number, it was the first time ermine scat had been recorded in Haida Gwaii, which gave him a starting point for his research. He was happy. Of all the technologies and techniques he had tried, using the dog had produced the most results. For Pips, poop hunting had been a great game. While Wijdeven got the evidence he so wanted for science, Pips won the prize he wanted for playing the game right—a chance to play with the ball!

Wijdeven learned that there were not many ermine in the area and could not come up with a scientifically accurate population estimate. However, he was able to confirm that, like other ermines in different locations, the Haida Gwaii critters were habitat generalists, which means that they use a variety of landscapes. He came to this conclusion because Pips had found droppings in all sorts of places—on the beach, near creeks, in old-growth forests and in younger ones.

Pips is one of many canines who have helped scientists detect the presence of an elusive animal in an area when other methods had failed. Other noninvasive tools such as remote cameras and hair snares have been used to confirm a species' presence, but detection dogs have been proven to offer a more effective and quicker way to find a species. A study published in 2018 compared the effectiveness and cost of three noninvasive techniques—scat detection dogs, remote cameras and hair snares—for finding black bears, fishers and bobcats in densely forested areas of Vermont. Researchers found that the dog teams were much more effective than either remote cameras or hair snares at detecting all three species. The second-best method was remote cameras, but the canines detected 3.5 times more

To this day, locating Haida Gwaii ermine scat is the toughest project Pips has worked on as a conservation canine. He had never come across a species as hard to detect as the ermine.

of each of the target species than the cameras did. Hair snares failed to detect either fishers or bobcats.

Another study conducted by the Conservation Canines group compared dogs' detection abilities to vocalization surveys for locating the endangered northern spotted owl in California. Before the dogs came in, researchers' main method of establishing the presence of northern spotted owls in a landscape was the owls' response to simulated calls. However, one of the most serious threats facing the northern spotted owl is the expansion of another closely related owl species, the barred owl. Because barred owls may attack northern spotted owls, the latter are known to vocalize less when the other species is around. This meant another survey technique had to be tried, because when repeated vocalization surveys indicate no vocal response from spotted owls for three consecutive years, the territory is considered unoccupied, and there is no more protection for the area. Detection dogs were brought in to locate owl pellets accumulated under roost sites. The dogs detected a significantly higher number of both spotted and barred owls than vocalization surveys had.

A northern spotted owl in California.

Collette Yee holds up a sample of orca feces that will be sent later to the lab for analysis.

POOP—HIDDEN TREASURE FOR SCIENTISTS

Poop is a real treasure for scientists. It contains a lot of valuable information about an animal's health, diet, stress levels, reproductive status and exposure to toxins and diseases. DNA can be extracted from scat to determine the species, the sex and even the individual identity of the animal that left the droppings. Based on the number and location of samples found in an area, researchers can learn more about the abundance of a species, how the animals are distributed in a geographic area, how they move, how far they travel, where they like to spend time and the size of their territory. They can determine whether an elusive species is present or absent in a landscape, understand the particular area a species prefers and discover the impact of human disturbances on the health of animals over time. Over the years, statistical and laboratory techniques have become more sophisticated, and the amount of data researchers have been able to extract from animal droppings has increased significantly. Fecal samples contain more and different information than what can be collected through other wildlife-detection methods, such as hair snares or remote cameras.

Imagine going to the doctor for an annual checkup. The doctor would get little information if only a strand of your hair were collected, but a blood test would answer all sorts of health-related questions. Scat provides the same information that a blood sample does. When researchers gather hair from an animal, they can confirm the species and the individual identity, but not information about its diet, territory preference and the other details that poop provides. Hiring a detection-dog team can be expensive, however, and if the canines aren't sent to the right area, they won't find any droppings. When possible, it is best for scientists to use a combination of methods to improve their chances of learning about a particular wildlife species.

Acquiring such information is important for making conservation decisions such as protecting an area as critical habitat of endangered wildlife or addressing threats an animal is facing, for example *pollution* or lack of food.

Dogs have been trained since the 1970s to identify and find the precious droppings from different species. With their super noses, they can make a difference in helping to protect fragile species that are running out of options. For example, a project run by Working Dogs for Conservation that relied on detection dogs to find the feces of the endangered San Joaquin kit fox provided the evidence that led to the development of new protected areas in the San Joaquin Valley in California. In Nepal and Vietnam, detection dogs have searched for pangolin droppings, which provide a genetic fingerprint that makes it possible to track illegal shipments of pangolins to the regions in which the animals were captured and thus home in on criminals. Pangolins are one of the world's most trafficked animals today because of their scales.

Heath Smith examines the droppings of a Haida Gwaii ermine. Poop contains a lot of valuable information about an animal's health, diet, stress levels, reproductive status and exposure to toxins and diseases.

Cheetah Conservation Fund detection-dog handler Quentin de Jager puts Levi through a series of daily exercises to sharpen skills and reinforce their bond.

DOGS TO THE RESCUE OF BIG CATS

In 2017, Levi, a Belgian Malinois/German shepherd cross, joined the Cheetah Conservation Fund to detect the scat of cheetahs, leopards and African wild dogs in Namibia. Levi is an experienced detection dog. Before going to Namibia for his new job, he was part of an anti-poaching team in South Africa, using his nose to detect rhino horn. "Dogs are the most effective tool we have against poaching, even with all the technology we have today," says Quentin de Jager, Levi's handler. "Nothing compares to what the dogs are capable of."

When it comes to detecting animal scat in the wild, de Jager is impressed by the ability of the canine nose. "The dogs will find 90 percent of the samples. Humans find 5 or 10 percent." In the field, when he says the word *soek*, which means "search" in Afrikaans, Levi runs around looking for cheetah scat. Once he finds it, he is rewarded with a ball to fetch.

In turn, researchers are rewarded with new information. In the CCF's genetics laboratory, they extract and analyze DNA to find out how many cheetahs are in an area and how they are distributed. Scat analysis also reveals information about their overall health, diet and even stress levels. In the past, farmers killed many cheetahs because they blamed them for attacking their livestock. Now researchers know what cheetahs eat, and they can show farmers that the felines are not always responsible for killing livestock. This helps reduce human-wildlife conflict and saves the lives of cheetahs.

Levi may have an exceptional nose, but he still has to work hard to earn his reward. In his past job, he searched for illegal wildlife products in small areas such as vehicles

Cheetahs are the fastest land animals on earth, but today they are struggling in a race against extinction.

Detection-dog handler Quentin de Jager and Levi. Detection dogs are important members of the Cheetah Conservation Fund's research team, as they find cheetah scat—called "black gold" by team members—in the field, enabling geneticists to study cheetah DNA noninvasively.

or public buses, but in Namibia it is different. He is tasked with looking for rare cheetah scat over huge areas, and the work can become a little frustrating when he doesn't find anything. De Jager's job is to help Levi maintain a positive attitude in the field even if there isn't any cheetah scat to find.

"It must be a fun game for him, and he must still enjoy searching," says de Jager. This is why he always keeps a few cheetah scat samples with him. When Levi cannot find anything in the field and his motivation is going down, de Jager hides a few samples so Levi can find them and get his ball reward. De Jager has trained Levi since he was a puppy and has a strong bond with his canine friend. "I trust my life with Levi in the field."

SNIFFING SCAT OUT AT SEA

One of the most unusual tasks detection canines have had to master is locating orca (killer whale) poop floating on the waters of Puget Sound off Washington State. The southern resident orca population, found in the northeast Pacific Ocean, was listed as endangered in 2001 under Canada's Species at Risk Act and in 2005 under the United States' Endangered Species Act. As of 2019, the population was only 73 animals.

One of the main reasons the orcas are not doing well is they do not have enough fish to eat. Unlike transient orca populations, which feed on marine mammals, southern residents eat mostly salmon. More than 95 percent of their diet consists of salmon, three-quarters of it Chinook. Unfortunately Chinook salmon populations have been declining. The southern residents are also endangered by increased boat traffic and the associated noise, and by

Collette Yee and Conservation Canine Dio are on a mission to find orca poop in Puget Sound, WA.

harmful human-made toxicants polluting the ocean, which accumulate in their bodies.

Scientists want to better understand the impacts of the boat traffic, pollution and lack of food so that more effective conservation measures can be implemented to save these endangered animals. However, it is difficult, time-consuming and invasive to collect tissue samples from marine mammals, especially within a small endangered population.

This is why researchers from University of Washington's Conservation Canines decided to call on dogs to sniff out orca poop at sea. Orca scat is difficult to see with human eyes. It can be very small, and it often sinks quickly. But

Collette Yee is by Dio's side as the dog sniffs for orca scat.

for trained detection dogs, this is not a problem. They can sniff it out at distances of up to one nautical mile, even in fast-moving currents.

Every year from early May until at least the end of October, conservation dogs help scientists track down the feces of the three southern resident orca pods, called J, K and L, that feed in the Salish Sea (the inland waters of Washington State and British Columbia) at that time of year. Dio was one of the dogs. An Australian cattle dog rescued from a shelter in California, he worked at the bow of a research vessel for two years in a row, dressed in a bright orange vest.

On a typical field day on the water, Collette Yee, Dio's handler, is by the dog's side, intensely focused on what Dio is "saying." Yee uses her hands to give instructions to Dr. Deborah Giles, a marine mammal scientist and the boat's captain. To make it easier for the dog to smell the orca poop, Giles positions the boat perpendicular to the wind and at least 400 yards (366 meters) downwind of an area the whales have just traveled. As the boat reaches the center of the scent cone, where the odor is the strongest, the dog becomes more agitated, moves across the bow, leans over the side of the boat and points with his head. Yee reads the cues from Dio and continues to instruct Giles to turn into the wind and make small adjustments left and right so the boat stays on the scent line until the scat is reached.

This is a tricky procedure that requires a more complex kind of teamwork. On land, detection dogs can show their human partner exactly where the poop is, but on a boat they aren't allowed to jump into the water to do that. They must clearly communicate what they have found without using much of their body to do so. "Sometimes it is really obvious. The dogs will start to pull themselves over the side of the boat, and they are whining or wagging their tails. But sometimes it is really subtle. They lick their lips and look around in certain ways," says Yee. "Every dog does it differently."

Giles moves the boat closer and closer to the scat until the team can retrieve it. "As the vessel driver, it is my job to take Dio where he wants to go, so I think of myself as being his legs," she says. As soon as the boat reaches the sample, team members scoop it up. They use a container attached to a long pole and skim the surface of the water just in front of the scat. The poop is shown to Dio, who immediately gets his reward—a game of catch and tug with his favorite ball and human on the bow of the boat. The samples are put on ice and will be sent later to the lab for analysis. Each scat collected takes the researchers a step closer to understanding what can be done to help the conservation of the orcas.

Not all detection dogs are a good fit for work on boats. Some canines have too much energy and get impatient

After finding the feces, Dio immediately gets his reward—a game with his favorite ball and Collette Yee, on the bow of the boat.

Southern resident orcas are endangered.

because they are not able to run on the boat as they would on land. Dio not only has strong sea legs but is also a very patient boy who knows how to communicate with his human handler. All these qualities make him ideally suited for working his nose on a boat.

In addition to collecting poop with the help of the dog, the field team is gathering other useful information about the orcas. They take photos of individual animals to see which whales are present. They count the number of boats and what type are near the whales, since noise from vessels is known to have a negative impact on the orcas.

Dogs have been looking for orca droppings for over a decade, but in the last few years the scat has become harder to find. The orcas are spread out over larger areas, looking for fish. Sometimes the researchers do not see them for days and days. And when the whales are present, the conditions have to be just perfect for Dio and his human team to find the orcas' poop. If it is too windy, the water becomes choppy, and the samples are easily destroyed.

Captain Deborah Giles positions the boat to make it easier for Dio to locate the scat scent.

If there isn't enough wind, the odor is not carried in the air, and the dog cannot smell it. Scat must float on the surface long enough for the researchers to collect it. And in order to float, it must contain sufficient fat. In recent years, because the orcas do not have enough to eat, they are not pooping very much, and the texture, color and size of the feces is different. When they have lots of fish to eat, their poop is fatty and much bigger. It floats at the surface for a long time, making it easier to collect. With fewer salmon for the orcas to feed on, their scat is smaller and almost chalky, becoming more dispersed and therefore more challenging to find.

Given the challenges of the study, researchers have collected an impressive number of samples, which has resulted in important science findings. Between 2008 and 2014 the dogs helped scientists collect 348 scat samples from 79 southern resident orcas. One of the most important findings from the analysis was that 69 percent of orca pregnancies had failed. The study linked the orcas' unsuccessful pregnancies to malnutrition and higher stress as a result of the lack of Chinook salmon. These findings are important to ensuring a future for the southern resident orcas. They show that it is critical to take action to recover Chinook salmon populations so that the orcas have enough to eat and can become healthier and able again to successfully give birth to calves.

In 2019 Yee and Dio left Conservation Canines to join Rogue Detection Teams. Giles was able to train her own dog, Eba, a rescue from the streets of Sacramento, to be the next whale-scat dog. That year they collected feces from not only southern resident orcas but also humpback whales and mammal-eating orcas.

Thanks to Dio's work, researchers are gathering important information that can be used to help conserve the southern resident orcas.

Koala populations are declining in Australia due to many threats.

DOG ON DUTY: SEARCHING FOR KOALAS

In 2015 researchers Celine Frere and Romane Cristescu founded Detection Dogs for Conservation at the University of the Sunshine Coast in Australia. They rescue, train, test and deploy canines to protect the unique wildlife of Australia, which is home to many threatened species. For example, koalas were classified as a vulnerable species in 2012 under the Australian government's Environment Protection and Biodiversity Conservation Act. The koala population is declining due to habitat loss and fragmentation, urban development, road mortality, domestic dog attacks and disease.

It is critical to monitor koala populations so that scientists can learn more about the challenges they face and better protect the animals.

The problem is, even though koalas are one of Australia's most well-known and charismatic wildlife species, they are actually hard to find in the field, not only because they have become rare but also because they are not easy to spot. They are well camouflaged by their environment, they do not move much—and when they do, they are quiet—and they often sit high in the dense foliage of trees.

This is where dogs trained to sniff out koala scat come to the rescue. One koala can produce 150 poops a day, so the dogs are kept busy. Cristescu conducted tests to investigate the accuracy and efficiency of a detection dog specifically trained for koala-scat surveys. She established that the canine found and indicated the location of koala poop 97 percent of the time and that the average time it took to locate the sample was 56 seconds. She also compared the dog's performance in a field survey to that of a human-only team. She found that the detection dog team was 19 times more time-efficient and 153 percent more accurate than the human-only team.

Using detection dogs, the researchers have proven that koalas can behave in surprising and unpredictable ways. For example, they found koalas right in the middle of urban areas, along roads that are now acting as corridors because they have the last remaining trees in agricultural landscapes.

When wildfires ravaged Australia in 2019–20, these special dogs were deployed to help locate injured, malnourished or isolated koalas after the fires left them without food or water in their destroyed habitat.

When he picks up the mussel scent and locates the sample, Seuss lies down, which is the passive alert he has been taught to give his human partner.

SNIFFING OUT INVASIVE SPECIES

Sometimes detection canines are hired to find something that is not wanted. Invasive species are the second-most significant threat to biodiversity after habitat loss. When humans go into the territory of wild animals, they may introduce plants and animals that do not belong in these places. Whether this happens accidentally or intentionally, the introduced species is capable of moving aggressively through an area and has the potential to compete with the native species, disrupting the natural balance that existed before the invader's introduction. Most species have predators in their natural habitat that keep their population in check, but when new species are introduced, they typically have no natural predators. They are often hardier, more aggressive and able to reproduce faster than the native species.

The best way to stop the spread of invasive species is to catch them early. Luckily, detection dogs excel at this job. While human searchers often cannot find intruders until after they have taken over and it is too late, dogs are able to smell the first colonizers, alerting wildlife managers to the early signs of an invasion. In different parts of the world, dogs have been trained to search for all kinds of non-native species, including animals, insects and plants.

SMALL SPECIES, BIG PROBLEM

Invasive zebra and quagga mussels can cause irreversible damage to water bodies and are difficult to get rid of when established.

Sometimes the tiniest species can pose the biggest threat. With an average length of 2 to 2.5 centimeters (about 1 inch), zebra and quagga mussels look harmless, but in reality they are one of the worst invasive species. They came from eastern Europe to the Great Lakes region of Canada and the United States in the late 1980s, catching a ride in the ballast water of cargo ships. Ballast water is held in the tanks and cargo holds of ships to provide stability and maneuverability. When a ship is receiving or delivering cargo at a port, it may release or take on a portion of ballast water. This water may contain non-native species such as zebra and quagga mussels.

Once the mussels arrive at a lake, it is not long before they take over the ecosystem, disrupting food webs and causing irreversible damage. They multiply rapidly, have no natural predators, release up to one million offspring per season and are difficult to get rid of once they are established. As filter feeders, they eat tiny phytoplankton in the water. In doing so, they take away the natural nutrients of the lake, which decreases the amount of food available for native fish species.

The mussels attach to any hard surface, such as boat hulls, buoys, ropes, trailers or motor equipment, and even to soft surfaces such as vegetation or a sandy bottom, which allows them to be moved easily between lakes. In addition to the damage they do to ecosystems, they may clog sewage-treatment facilities, water intakes and power-plant pipes, greatly increasing the maintenance costs of infrastructure.

MUSSEL-SNIFFING DOGS TO THE RESCUE

In Canada, the province of Alberta is mussel-free for now and wants to keep it that way. Indeed, if mussels were to invade Alberta, it would cost the province an estimated $75 million per year just to clean the infrastructure damaged by the mussels. To keep the tiny invaders at bay, the provincial government created the Aquatic Invasive Species Program. Watercraft inspections are a big part of this prevention effort. Cindy Sawchuk, who leads the program, thought that dogs could help win the battle, and

Cindy Sawchuk works alongside Hilo as he searches for dead zebra mussels, planted by the handlers for the dogs to find, along the shoreline of Upper Kananaskis Lake, AB.

Alberta became the first jurisdiction in Canada to employ detection canines for this job.

Since 2015 canines Hilo, Seuss and Diesel have worked with their human partners, Cindy Sawchuk, Hannah McKenzie and Heather McCubbin, to protect Alberta from a mussel invasion. Seuss and Diesel came from rescue shelters in the United States, while Hilo started out in guide-dog school in California.

In the summertime the province requires any watercraft—from stand-up paddleboards and kayaks to canoes and motorboats—to stop at a station where inspectors check them for unwanted species. The canines are there to

Hilo, Seuss and Diesel (left to right) are on the front lines in Alberta's battle to keep invasive mussels out of the province's waterways.

help, and they make the inspections a lot easier. "We can't see in all the nooks and crannies where the mussels like to hide, but to the dogs it doesn't matter if it is daytime or nighttime, they can still put their noses where their noses need to be," says Sawchuk.

"The dogs help us to be more certain that the boats we are allowing into the province are not carrying invasive species," says McKenzie.

Sawchuk and her team conducted a test in 2014 with canines from Working Dogs for Conservation to compare boat inspections done by humans versus inspections done by canines. In this blind trial, conducted at a used-boat shop, the dogs and humans individually inspected the same vessels, some of which had been planted with invasive mussels. They found that the dogs had 100 percent accuracy and that it took them 2.3 minutes to search a watercraft. Humans spent more than double that time and had only 75 percent accuracy.

The canines also help educate boat owners about the importance of cleaning their boats properly before moving them from one body of water to another, so that they do not transport invasive species. Boaters are even handed out collector cards, with photos of the dogs on them, that say, *You have been sniffed.*

Handler Hannah McKenzie rewards Seuss with a play session after he has found a zebra-mussel training sample on the shoreline.

These super canines are not only inspecting boats. They are also looking for mussels along shorelines at lakes and reservoirs, focusing on the popular water bodies of Alberta that are most at risk of mussel attacks because they attract a lot of boaters from outside the province.

One sunny day during the spring, Hilo, Seuss and Diesel are standing on the shore of Upper Kananaskis Lake. Clad in bright vests, they are patiently awaiting

Conservation canines such as Diesel have a very high play drive and are obsessed with the ball.

instructions from their handlers. The team is at this site to demonstrate the canines' detection skills, and the handlers have planted dead zebra mussels along the shoreline for the dogs to find.

The three canines are all business, noses to the ground as they search for the minuscule, well-camouflaged mussels. Seuss slowly moves along the shoreline. When he picks up the mussel scent and locates the sample, he locks eyes with his teammate, McKenzie, and sits down, which is the passive alert he has been taught to give. "Good job, Seuss, good boy. Awesome!" says McKenzie, who rewards the dog by tossing a ball from her belt pack. The dog excitedly runs off to fetch it.

"For the dogs, this work is a giant game," says Sawchuk. "The ball is their paycheck."

While to an outsider the job of working with a mussel-sniffing canine might seem straightforward, McKenzie, Sawchuk and McCubbin had to go through intensive training to learn how to work with dogs in the field.

"It is like learning a new language and a new dance all at the same time," McKenzie says. "You have to figure out what the dog is telling you and how to communicate what you want them to do. And you need to help them get their nose where it needs to be without getting in the way, without tripping on your own feet or getting entangled in the leash," she says. "I think the dogs learned their end of the job a lot faster than us humans."

In the field, the dogs have different ways of approaching the job. Hilo, a black Lab/golden retriever cross, is very methodical, while Seuss, an impressive 70-pound German shepherd, and Diesel, a chocolate Labrador, move quickly. "Seuss tends to rush more. It took a lot to teach him to

Protecting Alberta from a mussel invasion (left to right): canines Hilo, Diesel and Seuss and human partners Cindy Sawchuk, Heather McCubbin and Hannah McKenzie.

slow down, be more detailed and keep his nose on the ground to look for such a small target," McKenzie says.

Each dog lives with its handler and has developed a strong bond with them. When they are working together, the handler must learn to regulate their own emotions and set aside any negative feelings, because the dog easily picks up on its human partner's state of mind, which can hinder its ability to search. "If you have negative or unfocused emotions, it is a distraction to them. They realize something is wrong, and they don't want to play the game as much," McKenzie says.

While these dogs have been specifically trained to detect zebra mussels, they have also learned to search for other introduced species. They were used in a provincial park to detect an invasive weed, and they are now also detecting wild boar scat. By keeping unwanted invaders away, conservation dogs contribute to protecting native wildlife.

New Caledonian crows at Le Parc Zoologique et Forestier de la province Sud in Nouméa, New Caledonia.

FINDING CROW TOOLS

There is much about the animal world we still do not know, and canines' sniffing power can help advance scientific knowledge in many ways. Crows are intelligent creatures, and they have intrigued scientists for a long time. One crow species in particular, the New Caledonian crow, appears to be even smarter than average. Researchers have discovered that these birds, who are related to ravens, American crows and magpies, manufacture tools of a specific shape. They are the only species other than humans to do so.

Animals typically use only one type of tool. Sea otters, for example, bang shells with objects such as rocks to open them. Other birds, such as the Galapagos finch, pick up sticks and use them as is. New Caledonian crows take things a step further. They craft sticks into hooked tools that they use to probe for larvae and insects hidden in tiny holes in trees.

Natalie Uomini, a senior scientist at Germany's Max Planck Institute for the Science of Human History, wants to learn more about crows that make stick tools, and she is calling on sniffer dogs for a novel application of their smelling abilities. She has teamed up with Detection Dogs for Conservation at the University of the Sunshine Coast in Australia to bring canines into the thick forests of New Caledonia—the group of islands in the South Pacific where these particular crows live—to help locate the tools the crows have made.

When a crow makes a tool, it flies off into the forest with it, and researchers can rarely recover it. However, because crows leave some saliva on their tools, detection dogs can be trained to identify this scent and smell their way to the tools crows have left behind.

In order to train a dog to recognize the saliva, the researchers used Q-tips that zookeepers had swabbed inside captive crows' mouths. The canine correctly located the hidden Q-tips that had been in the crows' mouths and ignored the "clean" ones. After all the tests, Natalie and her team walked the dog around the forest. They found several sticks on the ground that were exactly the same size and shape as the crow tools they had seen before.

When researchers retrieve the tools, they can learn more about the birds' extraordinary skills and answer questions such as how far the crows travel with their tools, where they take them and how they make them.

A NOSE FOR POISON

In 2003 Samuel Infante saw one of the most heartbreaking scenes in his life. He was called to a farm in the center of Portugal where 33 griffon vultures, 3 cinereous vultures and 3 red kites (a kite is a bird of prey) had been poisoned after feeding on a sheep that had been laced with poison in order to control *feral* dogs. It was one of the worst incidents of wildlife poisoning ever recorded in Portugal. "It was terrible. I will never forget it," Infante says.

A lover of birds since he was a child, Infante became an ornithologist and founded a wildlife hospital in his hometown of Castelo Branco, which is located in the center of Portugal, about two hours away from Lisbon, the country's capital. Passionate about vultures, Infante had played an important role in bringing cinereous vultures back to Portugal, where they had been officially declared extinct. Witnessing the vultures being destroyed by poison was truly devastating for him. He knew that many farmers and hunters illegally used poison to kill wolves, dogs, foxes and even eagles and vultures that they viewed as either threats or, in the case of hunters, competition. He wanted to do everything he could to fight the poisoning of the wildlife he loved so much.

A member of Portugal's National Republican Guard, or Guarda Nacional Republicana, holds the carcass of a poisoned common buzzard.

POISON AND WILDLIFE

People in the Mediterranean region were using poison as far back as the fifth century BC. In Greece farmers used toxic plants to control wolves and other predators they considered threats to their livestock. Over the centuries this harmful practice has continued. Although the use of poison to kill wildlife is now forbidden in Europe, toxic substances are still available for people to purchase, and illegal poisoning continues today, especially as wolves, bears and other species return to Europe in higher numbers. Farmers place poison in livestock carcasses as bait to attract and kill wild animals. Poisoned bait has a large negative impact on overall biodiversity and wildlife. It is dangerous to people and pets, particularly when baits are left on roads and near villages, and it puts many endangered species at risk, particularly *scavengers* such as vultures, which feed on dead animals. Poisoned animals may also drink from rivers and wells and contaminate the water.

Many vulture species are endangered in Europe, including the Egyptian vulture and the cinereous vulture. As nature's garbage collectors, vultures play an important role in the environment. They clean up carcasses and recycle them into the ecosystem as nutrients, and they keep the environment clean and free of contagious diseases. These birds have an extremely corrosive stomach acid that allows them to consume rotting animal corpses. Scavenged leftovers are often infected with anthrax, botulinum toxins, rabies and hog cholera, which would kill other scavengers if left to rot. So by ridding the ground of dead animals, vultures prevent diseases from spreading to humans and animals.

A single poisoned carcass left in a field can result in hundreds of deaths. Some animals may survive, depending on the quantity and toxicity of the poison they have ingested and how quickly they are rescued. The lack of data on illegal poisoning makes it difficult to stop the practice. Between 2000 and 2010, more than 1,300 animals in Portugal died as a result of poisoning. Many incidents are not detected, as poisoned animals are not always taken to wildlife hospitals and so are not included in the

Veterinarian Ana Filipa handles a rescued griffon vulture at a wildlife hospital in Portugal.

official statistics. Researchers estimate that only 10 percent of wildlife poisonings are detected.

In order to address this crisis, the European Union's LIFE program supported an Innovation against Poison project between 2010 and 2014. The project experimented with ways to help stop illegal poisoning in three European countries, Portugal, Spain and Greece. Among other initiatives, the project employed a European Canine Team (ECT) to conduct annual inspections in the three participating countries. The dogs were trained to detect poisoned baits and carcasses in the field. Between 2011 and 2014, the ECT carried out 303 field inspections, locating 126 poisoned baits and 205 poisoned animals that otherwise would have gone undetected.

CANINES AGAINST POISON

Samuel Infante was one of the people involved in the European Union project. In 2012 he brought a team of dogs to Portugal from Spain for two weeks to search for poison in the field. Infante's goal was to show the Portuguese national environmental police that canines could be helpful in the fight against illegal poisonings. And the dogs didn't disappoint. They spent most of their time in International Tagus Natural Park (Parque Natural do Tejo Internacional), a biodiversity hot spot and a refuge for many threatened species, including the Iberian imperial eagle. The dogs found poison every day in that first year. The following year they did not find as much, and in 2014 there was no poison at all. Of course, poison is still used illegally in the region, but the canines did make a difference. The Portuguese police were impressed, and in 2015 they acquired their own dogs to do the job.

The Guarda Nacional Republicana engages German shepherds to detect poison in natural areas of Portugal.

The National Republican Guard, or GNR (Guarda Nacional Republicana), now has nine dogs located in different regions of the country.

Pico and Chico, both German shepherds, are part of this team. Their mission is to look for poison in Central Portugal, in Tagus National Park. Sometimes their handlers receive a tip from the police's environmental unit about a site they suspect has poison. Other times Pico and Chico just search various areas so that farmers and hunters are aware of their presence and no longer want to take the risk of using poison.

So far the dogs have been effective. The poisoned bait they find becomes important evidence police can use to open an investigation that, hopefully, leads to identifying and punishing the poisoner. But the dogs' biggest impact is that their presence in the region makes farmers and hunters

Poisoned bait found by the Guarda Nacional Republicana's canines is evidence police can use to identify and punish people who illegally poison wildlife. Dogs that search for poisoned bait are protected by a muzzle that acts as a barrier and prevents them from picking up the bait and being poisoned.

more likely to change their behavior. Since the canines have been involved, the police have been able to keep the natural park poison-free. "People talk in cafés, hunters talk among themselves, because they see the dogs. People now know the police have the tools to look for poison, so they change the way they do things," Infante explains. And now that the dogs are watching, Infante can continue to help cinereous vultures establish a stronger population in Portugal.

DOGS AGAINST WILDLIFE TRAFFICKING

Benny is at the Port of Tacoma in Washington State, surrounded by tall piles of colorful sealed shipping containers. He is eagerly awaiting Detective Lauren Wendt's signal. "Find it," she says. The black Labrador immediately gets to work, methodically and swiftly searching one container after another and following Wendt's hand. With his paws perched against the stacks, he sniffs and sniffs until he hits on a smell. He slows down, has a more thorough sniff and finally confirms his find by sitting down. "Good boy," Wendt says, retrieving the piece of elephant ivory she hid there earlier as part of a training exercise. Benny is immediately rewarded with a game of fetch with his favorite orange ball.

To Benny, the search is all about the game, but his work is serious business. Detective Wendt and K9 Benny work with the Washington Department of Fish and Wildlife Police to fight wildlife trafficking.

WILDLIFE FOR SALE

Wildlife trafficking is the selling of illegally obtained dead or living plants and animals and the products derived from them. Wildlife trafficking is pushing numerous species to

Detective Lauren Wendt and Labrador retriever Benny work together to help the Washington Department of Fish and Wildlife fight illegal wildlife trafficking.

Wildlife-detection dog Benny poses with various illegal products he helps detect—elephant ivory, rhino horns, bear gallbladders, shark fins, firearms and ammunition.

extinction, all around the world. Experts estimate revenue from black-market sales of endangered species and/or parts of them—tusks, pelts, horns and other body parts—to be in the billions of dollars annually.

Why do people want these species? Some animals, such as African gray parrots, Asian small-clawed otters and squirrel monkeys, are wanted as pets. Other species are desired for their meat, considered a delicacy in certain countries. Some animal parts are sought for fashion products such as handbags or shoes, or they are used in traditional Asian medicines.

Wildlife trafficking has a devastating impact on animals, causing huge declines in the populations of some of the world's most iconic species, as well as some of the lesser-known ones. It also results in the loss of global biodiversity. A study published in the journal *Science* in 2019 revealed that international wildlife trade was a factor in the endangerment of 958 species classified as threatened by the International Union for Conservation of Nature.

According to the wildlife-trade-monitoring organization Traffic, an estimated 1,000,000 pangolins were taken from the wild from 2000 through 2013. These shy animals are sought in Asia and Africa for their scales and body parts. They are the most illegally traded mammal in the world, and all eight species are now threatened with extinction. African elephants have also been heavily impacted by illegal trade—about 90 percent of them have been killed for their ivory tusks in the last 100 years. Between 2010 and 2012 alone, more than 100,000 elephants were killed in Africa.

In 1975 the Convention on Trade in Endangered Species of Wild Fauna and Flora was created to save species from overexploitation. So far 183 countries have signed the convention and have implemented laws to fight crimes against wildlife. However, the illegal killing of animals continues, including in national parks, as laws are not well enforced and countries lack the capacity to watch over large nature reserves. In many countries, local conservation groups work with governments to catch poachers, and patrol areas where the lives of animals such as rhinos and elephants are in danger. But to truly end wildlife trafficking, action must be taken to not only stop the people who take species from the wild but also discourage consumers from purchasing animals and animal parts around the world. Countries can make a difference by acknowledging that wildlife crime is a huge

Benny searches through cargo for items hidden by Washington Department of Fish and Wildlife detective Lauren Wendt.

Benny can search for illegal wildlife products a lot faster than a human can and with a higher degree of accuracy.

threat to biodiversity, enforcing local bans on wildlife trafficking and promoting public education campaigns.

A CERTIFIED FOUR-LEGGED DETECTIVE

With two of the busiest ports in the United States and a major international airport, Washington State is a target for the shipment of illegal wildlife parts. This is why in November 2015 Washington State voters overwhelmingly approved a law—known as the Washington Animal Trafficking Act (WATA)—that makes it illegal to buy, sell, trade and otherwise distribute parts or products from the 10 endangered animals most often illegally traded: elephants, rhinoceroses, lions, tigers, leopards, cheetahs, pangolins, marine turtles, sharks and rays. The law, which took effect in 2016, makes wildlife trafficking a felony in Washington State and allows the Washington Department of Fish and Wildlife Police to enforce penalties for traffickers who trade endangered species within the state of Washington.

Laws such as WATA help reduce the trafficking of animal products locally by making some people think twice about their actions, holding traffickers accountable if they are caught, and by creating public awareness. These laws send a message to the world that countries recognize wildlife trafficking as a global threat to be taken seriously. As such, they have an impact and help save species in the wild.

The Washington Department of Fish and Wildlife Police employs detectives who normally specialize in investigating illegal trade in local natural resources such as geoduck, crab, salmon, sturgeon, reptile species and bear parts.

Staff were not used to searching for illegal wildlife products coming from other countries, and to enforce

Detective Lauren Wendt and Benny take a break after a training exercise at the Port of Tacoma in Washington State.

the new law the department needed a fresh approach. Detective Lauren Wendt grew up with dogs in northern California, and she had been interested in preventing wildlife trafficking since she graduated from university with a wildlife management degree. She approached her employer with the idea of using a four-legged weapon against wildlife trafficking. Benny became the state's first wildlife-crime detection dog.

Wendt collaborated with Working Dogs for Conservation to find a suitable canine candidate for the job. She searched the internet for a rescue dog who had high energy and an obsessive play drive, the prime features of detection canines. She found a 16-month-old black Labrador retriever, located in northern California, who had too much energy for his owners and needed a new home. After being evaluated, the dog was determined to be a match for his new mission of fighting wildlife trafficking, and in May 2017 Benny was officially paired with Wendt. "His original name was Bandit," she says. "But I didn't really like that name for a police dog, so I came up with the name Benny."

Benny's expert nose helps wildlife officers seize some of the illegally trafficked animal products that pass through Washington State ports of entry.

Since his adoption the pair has spent countless hours working together. Wendt trains Benny on new scents by hiding a target odor—such as a piece of rhino horn or elephant ivory—in a small wooden box. She places that box in a row of identical boxes that have no scent. Benny is asked to "find it," and he is rewarded with his favorite toy if he sniffs out the scented box. Wendt uses a clicker or simple words to communicate with the dog. "The sound needs to be consistent and concise so the dog knows that every time they hear that specific sound, whatever behavior they were doing at that moment is correct and they are going to get a reward," Wendt says.

Illegally obtained fish and wildlife parts and products are transported to Washington State from other countries via air, ship or mail and can be disguised in many ways, making it difficult for officers to detect them. Smugglers may also hide animals or their parts on passengers on airplanes. It is extremely time-consuming for humans to inspect shipments by hand and try to determine the contents of packages. But for a master sniffer like Benny, it is easy. He can search a large area or multiple items a lot faster than a human could and with a higher degree of accuracy.

As part of his training routine, Benny is tasked to locate a target in a row of identical boxes.

Benny's nose helps wildlife officers seize some of the illegally trafficked animal products that pass through the state's ports of entry, from elephant ivory and bear gallbladders to rhino horns and shark fins. He can also detect firearms and spent casings, and he serves both state and federal wildlife agencies. For example, the federal Fish and Wildlife Service has called on Benny and Wendt to inspect shipments of wildlife for illegal products.

Benny has also helped local enforcement agencies search for firearms and spent ammunition in urban areas, whether the weapons were used in crimes related to poaching or not.

When Benny and Wendt are not working together on crimes related to wildlife, they visit schools and attend community events to educate the public about wildlife trafficking and how people can be part of the fight against it. In September 2019 Wendt and Benny left the Washington Department of Fish and Wildlife to work with the organization Working Dogs for Conservation in Montana, but Benny's legacy lives on in Washington State. The Woodland Park Zoo in Seattle has a dedicated wildlife-trafficking exhibit that includes a life-size statue of Benny.

Around the world, sniffer canines like Benny continue to help fight the trade in endangered wildlife. Dogs have become an important weapon in the fight against elephant and rhino poaching in various African countries, where they work to identify both animals and criminals, getting the scent of poachers from crime scenes. Whether those brave canines are in African nature reserves and parks or in North America's airports and ports, they work hard with their noses to help save endangered wildlife.

Benny poses next to his statue at Woodland Park Zoo's wildlife-trafficking exhibit in Seattle.

German shepherd Bar was born in Slovakia and is now Conservation Lower Zambezi's best tracker dog. He is posing with (left to right) Wildlife Rangers Adamson Phiri, Chris Sheleni, Sheleni Phiri (Bar's primary handler) and Peter Tembo. FRANÇOIS D'ELBÉE

A CANINE UNIT TO COMBAT WILDLIFE CRIME IN AFRICA

Conservation Lower Zambezi (CLZ) is a nonprofit organization that works alongside the local wildlife authority, the Department of National Parks and Wildlife, to protect vulnerable wildlife in Zambia. The Lower Zambezi National Park supports populations of iconic African species such as elephants, lions and leopards.

Like many other groups in Africa that employ sniffer dogs to combat wildlife poaching, CLZ set up a canine unit in May 2016 in response to an increase in elephant poaching. "Illegal wildlife trafficking is becoming more and more sophisticated in the way contraband is being moved," says Ian Stevenson, the organization's CEO. "It's hard to pick up wildlife products like elephant ivory when they are in a suitcase or in a car, so there was a need for us to get more sophisticated, and the dogs were one way to do that."

The K9 detection and tracking unit is made up of four handlers and three dogs. Their mission is to sniff out illegal wildlife products and track poachers, but they also act as deterrents. "We wanted people in the communities to know what these dogs can do, that they can easily find illegal items like ivory or firearms," says Stevenson. The dogs can identify elephant ivory, pangolin scales, rhino horn, bushmeat, cat skins—including leopards, lions and cheetahs—firearms and ammunition. They and their handlers are deployed to detect these products when vehicles, buses, buildings or villages are searched. The dog unit is tasked with helping protect the Lower Zambezi National Park and surrounding areas—about 7,722 square miles (20,000 square kilometers) in total.

Since the unit was formed, it has led to the successful arrest of many suspects and the confiscation of a high number of illegal wildlife products. For example, an informant may tell wildlife officers that a pangolin is being held somewhere in a village, but the officers cannot find it anywhere. When the dogs are let off leash to do a free search, running around the village and checking piles of grass, wood and trees, they can easily find it. "People will not always hide it in their houses but in the vicinity outside, so we use the dogs, and they are very successful at picking it up," Stevenson says.

The dogs regularly check buses for illegal wildlife products—they can search more buses, and a lot faster, than any human could. They can find ivory packed at the bottom of a suitcase on a bus. "There is no way a human would have ever picked it up," says Stevenson. Sometimes the zealous canines catch more than ivory. They may come away with an untargeted yet tasty find, such as one of the live chickens that bus passengers sometimes carry with them. "You put a dog in there, and you end up with one less chicken."

Handlers constantly look after their dedicated four-legged partners, who are so driven to work that they could kill themselves as they run around looking for something. In the hot climate of Zambia, the dogs can overheat, so their handlers monitor their temperatures and make sure the dogs don't overwork themselves. They carry ice packs for emergencies. The job is dangerous at times: one of the dogs, Lego, passed away in July 2019 due to suspected poisoning.

Lego was one of the first two dogs in the unit. He and Bar, German shepherds from the Netherlands, were trained by Invictus K9, a specialized group based in the United States that trains canines and handlers for the war on wildlife crime. Lego had contributed to the arrest of 82 poachers and the confiscation of 12 pieces of ivory, 40 firearms and more than 2,000 pounds (960 kilograms) of bushmeat. CLZ brought in two new Malinois dogs, Kalo and Amor, in March 2020 to continue and grow the program. Bar remains part of the team.

Handlers are recruited from the local communities and are trained for three months. Even if they have never had experience with dogs before joining the program, they become deeply bonded with their new canine partners. "You see the handlers and the dogs sitting on a stone overlooking the Zambezi, chatting with each other—this is something these guys never had before, never dreamed of having this relationship with an animal," says Stevenson. "They take care of these dogs like they are family."

Detection dog Amor, also known as Hammer, is having a grooming session with his primary handler, Wildlife Ranger Sunday Kaonga. Amor was born in Slovakia and started working for Conservation Lower Zambezi in 2020. MICHAEL HENSMAN (INVICTUS K9 & CONSERVATION LOWER ZAMBEZI)

The public gets a chance to meet the brand-new graduates of the 2019 K9 Major Memorial School in downtown Indianapolis, IN.

5

DOGS AND HUMANS: PARTNERS IN CONSERVATION

Every day, canines are working on the front lines of conservation, helping scientists and conservationists around the world understand and protect wildlife at risk. There seems to be no job too big for them, and these hard-working dogs are up for any challenge.

Conservation canines also give us the important message that we can do our part to protect our planet's biodiversity. Dogs make the world better and can inspire us to do so too. Children can become involved directly or indirectly to support what conservation dogs do by being responsible environmental stewards, contributing data to science, supporting animal shelters, engaging with dogs in their daily lives and more.

WHAT YOU CAN DO TO HELP CONSERVATION CANINES
JOIN THE DOGS IN MAKING A DIFFERENCE

- **Protect habitat for wildlife.** You can help support conservation dogs and the scientists who work with them by taking steps in your daily life to protect nature. One of the most important jobs of conservation dogs is to locate species in habitats that are increasingly at risk of being lost, so that wildlife managers can collect the data they need to conserve more habitat for the wildlife populations that need it. You can join the canines in making a difference and take action to protect natural habitats for species that live close to you or far away. For example, you could connect with a local nature group involved in restoring a degraded wetland or help plant local vegetation that provides cover for various wildlife. You can help protect endangered wildlife by changing things about the way you live—for example, buy and use less, and reuse and recycle as much as you can. These steps help cut down on pollution and also preserve wildlife habitats around the world.

Wildlife-detection dog Benny is trained to locate different types of illegal wildlife products, including shark fins.

- **Keep out the unwanted**. Many detection canines are involved in fighting invasive species. You can support them by becoming part of an environmental group's efforts to remove invasive plants in a local ecosystem. If your parents own a boat, you can help them clean their equipment so that invasive organisms are not introduced to the aquatic environment by accident.

- **Say no to wildlife trafficking**. Canines are at the forefront of one of the toughest and most dangerous conservation battles—protecting species from illegal poaching. When you are on holiday, be aware that many tourist products, such as ivory, tortoiseshell, coral and fur, are made from threatened species. Never ever buy animal products you suspect might be illegal. Keep your eyes open for signs of wildlife crime where you live. Your sighting of elephant ivory or rhino horn in a gift shop or antique store can help the local wildlife police enforce laws and stop traffickers. Make wildlife crime a topic of research and action in your

environmental club at school or with your friends in order to raise awareness of the need for stronger laws to fight wildlife trafficking. Do not buy or release exotic animals— they are not meant to be pets. Do not support local pet stores that sell exotic animals that belong in the wild.

• **Be a citizen scientist.** Dogs' amazing sense of smell helps scientists answer tough conservation questions by leading them to sources of data they would not have access to otherwise. You can join the ranks of these motivated four-legged *citizen scientists* and contribute to building the knowledge researchers need to better protect species. You can learn to become a citizen scientist yourself by joining a local nature club where you can participate in wildlife surveys and monitor wildlife, or you can contribute data to programs such as the Christmas Bird Count and the Great Backyard Bird Count.

Great Pyrenees are not only vigilant livestock guardian dogs but can also be wonderful companions to humans.

SUPPORT GROUPS THAT TRAIN AND EMPLOY CONSERVATION CANINES

It takes a lot of money to train one detection dog and the handlers who work with them. Find out more about the organizations that employ conservation canines around the world and what they need. You can organize fundraising events at your school or in your community to support the work that dogs do. For example, donations to Working Dogs for Conservation help them feed working dogs; purchase field vests, leashes and toy rewards; support dogs and handlers in the field; or screen shelter dogs as potential detection canines. Donations to Detection Dogs for Conservation can help cover the veterinary costs associated with keeping the dogs healthy, pay for a bed so the dogs can rest in the field, or contribute to the purchase of specialty booties to protect the dogs from injuring their paws on spikes, cacti or other hazards.

Many of the organizations that employ conservation canines team up with animal shelters to rescue dogs who cannot be adopted but have the qualities required to be excellent conservation workers. If you know of a dog in your community that might make a great conservation dog, you can notify groups such as Rescues 2the Rescue or Rogue Detection Teams, which match high-energy dogs to suitable working careers and hire them for conservation purposes.

Many groups have websites and social media pages where you can follow the adventures of their hardworking and passionate conservation canines in the field. The Rogue Detection Teams group regularly shares news about its dogs on various online platforms, and photos of its canines are posted on its website. You can show your support and love by sharing information and helping spread the word about these dedicated four-legged workers.

CONNECTING WITH DOGS IN YOUR COMMUNITY
HELP UNWANTED DOGS

Many canines on the front lines of wildlife conservation were once unwanted and in shelters. Conservation groups rescue dogs that have a hard time finding a home or cannot be adopted as pets. In giving these dogs a new purpose, people not only save their lives, but also give them a chance to save other animals. Unfortunately many dogs do not get this second chance. They either are strays or live out their lives in shelters. The American Society for the Prevention of Cruelty to Animals estimates that approximately 3.3 million dogs enter animal shelters in the United States every year. About 670,000 shelter dogs are euthanized annually.

A veterinary student from the University of Calgary shows a young dog owner how to perform a health examination during a traveling vet-clinic program in Tulita, a hamlet in the Sahtu Region of the Northwest Territories.

You can get involved and help improve the lives of shelter dogs. While some shelters require volunteers to be at least 16 years old to work directly with the animals, you can still help in many other ways. For example, you can collect towels and blankets for the animals, create and donate toys, participate in community events organized by the local shelter or offer to take dogs for a walk (supervised by your parents). You can also become an animal advocate and support laws that protect pets from abuse and cruelty. These are all great opportunities to not only help out dogs in need but also get to know about the animals and how to care for them.

UNDERSTAND THE CANINES IN YOUR LIFE

One of the best ways to learn about conservation canines is to understand dogs and be with them in your own community. If you don't have a dog at home, you can walk a neighbor's dog, spend time with friends who have dogs and offer to dog-sit for them, or just head to a local dog park and watch how dogs behave, communicate, play and interact with other dogs. You can learn about their emotions and discover what they like and don't like by paying attention to what makes each dog unique.

You don't have to travel into the field and see the special dogs that serve as conservation biologists tracking rare species and sniffing out endangered animal poop or illegal wildlife products. All dogs love to use their nose, and you can witness their extraordinary sniffing abilities in your daily life. Through your observations, you will learn how they use all their senses to understand their world, just as conservation canines do.

A child interacts with a dog available for adoption at the British Columbia Society for the Prevention of Cruelty to Animals.

Scientist Marc Bekoff, who wrote the book *Canine Confidential: Why Dogs Do What They Do*, loves to visit dog parks, which he describes as wonderful places for the study of animal minds and human-animal interactions. Observing dogs at the dog park is an opportunity to become a citizen scientist by learning to record animal behaviors.

After all, primatologist and conservationist Jane Goodall says that her memories of childhood are "almost inseparable from memories of Rusty," her dog. "He was my constant companion, and he taught me so much about the true nature of animals," she writes in *Reason for Hope*, the book she co-authored with Phillip Berman. A dog may change your life and inspire you to become a scientist!

And if you and your parents are considering a canine companion for your family, or already have one, be sure you are able to meet the needs of your dog. Think about how you can use your observations of dog behavior to be a better companion to them.

A child spends time with a puppy in Pond Inlet, NU.

The dog is a valued member of this family in the village of Kyuquot, BC.

Detective Lauren Wendt demonstrates Benny's powerful scent-detection abilities during a public event at Woodland Park Zoo in Seattle.

You don't have to own a trained detection dog to see a dog's nose in action. After all, canines are smelling machines, and you can engage in fun and easy activities at home with your dog to unleash their scent-detection skills. The National Association of Canine Scent Work runs the K9 Nose Work program, which gives pet dogs and their people a fun and easy way to learn these skills. The program is based on the principle that while some breeds are known to possess stronger sniffer skills than others, every dog has a nose far more amazing than any human's, along with the natural instinct to use it. In the K9 Nose Work program, dogs learn how to search for a specific odor and find the source. It starts with getting your dog excited about using its nose to search for its favorite hidden food or toy. Put the item to be found in a variety of places. Over time you can add new search skills, as long as you keep it fun and exciting for your canine buddy. This is a great way to play together while getting your dog to burn energy and gain increased focus and confidence. And if you and your dog enjoy the activities, you can take classes and even join competitions.

CITIZEN SCIENCE WITH YOUR DOG

In Australia the group Canidae Development specializes in working with canines to collect data for government, industry and nonprofit organizations through projects that make a difference in the environment. Canidae Development has been working with the Conservation Ecology Centre, which is dedicated to protecting and understanding Australian ecosystems and is based in the Great Ocean Road region of Australia, alongside Great Otway National Park. The team has developed a program called Otway Conservation Dogs to sniff out the endangered species of the region. What's unique about this project is that local community volunteers have been trained to work with their own dogs of various breeds to detect the scat of threatened species. They were particularly focused on finding the scat of the tiger quoll, the largest marsupial carnivore surviving on mainland Australia.

The country is home to four species of quolls. Quolls were among the first native animals described by European scientists. Unfortunately all quoll species have declined since European settlement, due to habitat loss and introduced predators such as foxes.

The tiger quoll is much larger than other species and has white spots that extend along its tail. Historically the tiger quoll was present throughout southeastern Queensland, eastern New South Wales, Victoria, southeastern South Australia and Tasmania. Now it is rare in southeastern Queensland and mainly restricted to national parks. In Victoria, its population has declined by nearly 50 percent.

When tiger quolls were rediscovered in the Otway region in 2012, there was a need to better understand them in order to implement effective conservation efforts, such as controlling invasive species. Employing citizen scientists and their pet dogs to find quoll scat was a great way to help protect this vulnerable species in the long term. Ten dogs and their owners participated in the program, which ran for five years. While this volunteer program no longer exists, Luke Edwards from Canidae Development still volunteers his time to conduct surveys with his dog Uda. Quolls are elusive, and their home ranges can be as large as 500 hectares (1,234 acres). Several extensive remote-camera surveillance programs had failed to capture an image, but Edwards and the volunteer team managed to find a few droppings.

Luke Edwards of Canidae Development and border collie Uda are about to begin a search in the Otways in southern Victoria, Australia. CHRISTOPHER JOYCE

Spending time in nature has tremendous benefits. Studies show that people who spend time at beaches, local parks or in the woods are healthier and happier than those who don't. Dogs are always excited about going outside, so they make great companions for enjoying the natural world. Because dogs sniff everything along the way, you can just let your four-legged companion be your guide and explore the natural world in ways you haven't before. Pay attention to the dog. What is it "seeing" with its nose? When you follow the dog's cues, you can become a real nature detective, noticing animals you may not have seen otherwise or spotting signs of wildlife such as tracks on a trail. Take along a naturalist's guide to help you identify different wildlife clues.

When exploring nature with a dog and your family, follow the rules. In some parks and natural areas, dogs are not permitted at all, so before heading out on a nature walk, make sure your dog is allowed on the trail. While walking, be curious and take notice of the habitat that wildlife species live in, but never disturb animals or their homes. Watch animals from a distance and always keep the dog on a leash, as unleashed dogs can chase and disrupt wildlife, destroy sensitive habitat and trample on plants.

LOOKING TO THE FUTURE

As humans' best friends, dogs lend their paws and noses to fixing some of the most complex environmental problems that we have imposed on the planet. They fight the invasive species that people have introduced to new environments. They combat the illegal poaching and trafficking of endangered species such as rhinoceroses and elephants.

Marshall and his dog, Tampa, pose in their home community of Tulita, a hamlet in the Sahtu Region of the Northwest Territories.

They track rare species in diminishing and fragmented habitats. They help people coexist with wild animals by protecting livestock, and they help find evidence of the negative impacts of human activities on the environment by retrieving the carcasses of birds and bats that have been hit by wind turbines. They work in all climates and can detect almost anything. They sniff out polar bear dens under the snow near areas being explored for oil and gas development, and identify the presence of harmful chemicals such as PCBs (polychlorinated biphenyls) in urban areas. In all these cases, canines' extraordinary abilities give wildlife managers the important information they need to protect habitat and wildlife.

Following the lead of these four-legged heroes, you can be a nature steward and a partner in conservation with your own dog and other animal friends in your life and community, and take action for the natural world.

Julianne Ubigau conducts a training session with long-time canine partner Casey, from the University of Washington's Conservation Canines program.

GLOSSARY

alert—a signal or notification. Tracking dogs give their handler an alert when they have successfully detected the target.

amphibians—vertebrates (animals with a backbone) that are born in water and breathe with gills, then develop into adults that breathe air through lungs and live on land and in water. Examples include frogs, toads, newts and salamanders.

bait—food put out to attract animals

biodiversity—the variety of life in a geographic region or ecosystem. An area with many different kinds of plants and animals is said to have high biodiversity, indicating a healthy ecosystem.

bond—form a close, strong, meaningful, long-lasting attachment

breeds—groups of animals within a species that have a distinctive appearance and particular characteristics, usually developed by careful selection

canine—dog or doglike, from canis, the Latin word for *dog*, and caninus (*of the dog*). Canine is also the large tooth between the incisors and the premolars, used for gripping prey.

carnivore—an animal that feeds on meat

citizen scientist—a member of the general public who collects scientific data, often in collaboration with or under the direction of professional scientists and scientific institutions

conservationist—a person who works to protect or conserve wildlife and the environment

den—the retreat or resting place of a wild animal

DNA—deoxyribonucleic acid, the material that carries all the information about how a living thing looks and functions. Each piece of information is carried on a different section of the DNA. These sections are called genes.

domestication—the process, which happens over many generations, of changing a wild animal into a tame one that can live with humans

ecosystem—a complex network involving all living organisms interacting with the nonliving components of their environment

endangered species—a plant or animal species existing in such small numbers that it is in danger of becoming extinct in the wild

extinction—the disappearance of a species from Earth

feral—not domesticated or having escaped domestication and become wild, such as feral cats

habitat—the natural place where plants, animals and other organisms are most suited to live and breed

herding—keeping or moving animals together. A herding dog is trained to help control and direct herds of cows, sheep or other livestock to a pasture or to a barn or other enclosure by nipping at them, barking or circling around them.

introduced species—an organism that has been accidentally or deliberately transported to a new location by human activity

invasive species—plants and animals from other places that are not native to a particular area and cause harm to the local environment and to the plants and animals that *are* native to the area

K9—homophone for *canine* that likely originated in World War II and was subsequently adopted by police departments and others working with dogs

livestock guardian dogs—dogs that have been specially bred to protect livestock from predators

native species—species that occur naturally in a particular area or habitat

olfactory—relating to the sense of smell

olfactory epithelium—a specialized membrane of tissue that lines the nasal cavity and contains olfactory receptor cells

pack—a group of animals of the same kind. The animals usually live together and hunt cooperatively, and they may be related.

poaching—the illegal catching or killing of an animal on someone else's land in contravention of official protection

pollution—the presence of harmful chemicals or other substances in the environment

predators—animals that hunt other animals for food

prey—an animal that is hunted and eaten by other animals

range—the native geographic area in which an organism can be found—the geographic distribution of a particular species

receptors—organs or cells in an animal's body that can respond to sensory signals such as light, smell or sound

scavenger—an animal that feeds on animal remains that it steals or finds or on garbage left out by humans

socialization—the process of preparing a dog to enjoy interactions and be comfortable with other animals, people, places, sounds and activities

species—a group of closely related organisms that share similar characteristics and are capable of producing offspring

transhumance—the seasonal migration of livestock to suitable grazing grounds

wetland—a land area where the soil is permanently or seasonally saturated with water

wildlife trafficking—the taking and selling of wild animals and plants and the products derived from them

Detection canine Seuss is rewarded with playtime in the water after his hard work at Upper Kananaskis Lake, AB.

RESOURCES

Print

Bekoff, Marc. *Canine Confidential: Why Dogs Do What They Do*. Chicago: University of Chicago Press, 2018.

Frydenborg, Kay. *A Dog in the Cave: The Wolves Who Made Us Human*. New York: HMH Books for Young Readers, 2017.

Hare, Brian, and Vanessa Woods. *The Genius of Dogs: How Dogs Are Smarter Than You Think*. New York: Penguin Group, 2013.

Horowitz, Alexandra. *Inside of a Dog: What Dogs See, Smell, and Know—Young Readers Edition*. New York: Simon & Schuster, 2017.

Horowitz, Alexandra. *Our Dogs, Ourselves: How We Live with Dogs—Young Readers Edition*. New York: Simon & Schuster, 2020.

Miklósi, Ádám. *The Dog: A Natural History*. Princeton, NJ: Princeton University Press, 2018.

Young, Jon, and Tiffany Morgan. *Animal Tracking Basics*. Mechanicsburg, PA: Stackpole Books, 2007.

Online

American Society for the Prevention of Cruelty to Animals: aspca.org

Canidae Development: canidaedevelopment.com.au

Conservation Canines: washington.edu/conservationbiology/conservation-canines

Detection Dogs for Conservation: usc.edu.au/research-and-innovation/animal-and-marine-ecology/detection-dogs-for-conservation

Hike with Your Dog: hikewithyourdog.com

Humane Society of the United States: hsus.org

International Union for Conservation of Nature's Red List of Threatened Species: iucnredlist.org

National Association of Canine Scent Work: nacsw.net

New Zealand Conservation Dogs Programme: doc.govt.nz/our-work/conservation-dog-programme

Rescues 2the Rescue: rescues2therescue.org

Rogue Detection Teams: roguedogs.org

TRAFFIC: traffic.org

Wind River Bear Institute: beardogs.org

Working Dogs for Conservation: wd4c.org

For a complete list of references, visit the page for this book at orcabook.com.

Links to external resources are for personal and/or educational use only and are provided in good faith without any express or implied warranty. There is no guarantee given as to the accuracy or currency of any individual item. The author and publisher provide links as a service to readers. This does not imply any endorsement by the author or publisher of any of the content accessed through these links.

ACKNOWLEDGMENTS

I am very grateful to the conservation canines who so graciously allowed me to follow them in the field. They showed a level of enthusiasm, energy and dedication in helping me tell their stories that I had rarely encountered before with any interview subjects. They were always patient, they happily let me photograph them, and they constantly encouraged me with wagging tails. I admire their commitment to field conservation. I deeply value the time I was able to spend with all the individuals who work alongside these amazing dogs and generously allowed me to join them in the field, letting me experience the unique bond they have with their canine partners, and shared their knowledge and experience. This book would not have been possible without these wonderful collaborations.

My thanks go out to Heath Smith, Jennifer Hartman, Collette Yee and Rita Santos of Rogue Detection Teams; Laurie Marker, founder and executive director of the Cheetah Conservation Fund, and her team; Silvia Ribeiro of Grupo Lobo and all the farmers who welcomed me to their land; Samuel Infante of Quercus and the CERAS team; Carrie Hunt and Nils Pedersen of the Wind River Bear Institute; Mathieu Mauriès; Raymonde Etcharry and Alain Domini; Cindy Sawchuk, Hannah McKenzie and Heather McCubbin of Alberta Environment and Parks; Lauren Wendt of Working Dogs for Conservation and the Washington Department of Fish and Wildlife; Anne Wallis and Patricia Corbett of Deakin University; Jeffrey Milner of the Indiana Department of Natural Resources; Deborah Giles of Wild Orca; Julianne Ubigau of the Center for Conservation Biology at the University of Washington; Luke Edwards of Canidae Development; Pete Coppolillo of Working Dogs for Conservation; Lynette Shimek; Ian Stevenson of Conservation Lower Zambezi; Romane Cristescu of Detection Dogs for Conservation at the University of the Sunshine Coast; Berry Wijdeven of the British Columbia Ministry of Forests, Lands, Natural Resource Operations and Rural Development; Tory Rhoads and Karen Blejwas of the Alaska Department of Fish and Game; Flossy Sperring of Earthcare St Kilda; Joshua Said of Dingo Den Animal Rescue; Gary Allan of Tundra Speaks; the Woodland Park Zoo; Le Parc Zoologique et Forestier de la province Sud in Nouméa, New Caledonia; and the National Republican Guard Canine Team.

I also thank Natalie Uomini and Juliane Bräuer of the Max Planck Institute for the Science of Human History; Linda van Bommel of the Australian National University; Nathaniel J. Hall of the Canine Olfaction Research and Education Laboratory at Texas Tech University; Adrian Treves of the Carnivore Coexistence Lab at the University of Wisconsin–Madison; and Aerin Jacob of the Yellowstone to Yukon Conservation Initiative. I am grateful to them all for contributing their expert insights and reviewing different parts of the text.

I thank Orca Book Publishers for supporting a book on conservation canines, and particularly my wonderful editor, Sarah Harvey, for her insightful comments, endless patience, support and love of dogs; Kirstie Hudson; and Dahlia Yuen for her beautiful design.

Deepest thanks and love to my family, my two children, Elodie and Emile, who joined me on several trips and met some of the dogs; my parents, who continually supported me with their enthusiasm; Lesley, who read my work and constantly shared her love of dogs; and my cat, Felicie, who often sat by my computer, watching dog photos with great calmness and patience.

INDEX

Page numbers in **bold** *indicate an image caption.*

ISABELLE GROC is a writer, conservation photographer and filmmaker who specializes in wildlife conservation, endangered species and the relationships between people and wildlife in a rapidly changing world. With degrees in journalism from Columbia University and urban planning from the Massachusetts Institute of Technology, she brings a unique perspective to documenting the impacts of human activities on threatened species and habitats. She is the author of *Gone Is Gone: Wildlife Under Threat* and *Sea Otters: A Survival Story* in the Orca Wild series. Born in the South of France, with family roots in Spain, Isabelle now lives in Vancouver.